KEEPING YOUR EYE ON THE FUTURE

INSIDE THE MIND OF A MOTIVATED TEEN

Second Edition

By George Alan Day

CreateSpace 2013

Acknowledgment

Accomplishing a goal is not a one-person deal. It is a team effort involving the help of our parents, teachers or instructors, friends, and most importantly God. I couldn't have done what I did alone. I am thankful for all those people who encouraged me to walk the high road and not just settle for less. I am thankful for those who didn't see me as a boy with a disability but rather as any other person who needed some work. I thrived on feeling normal not set apart. A special thanks to: Travis Tolbert, Sensei Kelly Rhodes, Ms. Sarah Landrenea (COLA Swimming Instructor), Nate Pry, Jacob Azennne, Katie Jones, Mike Ford, Michael Day, Conrad Roesky, Beverly Spell, Bob and Denise Shaner and family, and all the doctors and physical and occupational therapists who have assisted me on my journey. In addition to my friends, I especially thank my parents Alan and Michele Day, and my sisters Emily and Cecelia Day. My parents and sisters were and continue to be a great support, helping me to believe throughout my life that I'm not disabled and that *"I can do ALL things through Christ who strengthens me"*. (Philippians 4:13)

Parasailing with my Aunt Joan

Strengthening my body through karate

Chapter Index

Foreword

At 16, I have overcome the obstacles of Cerebral Palsy and a learning challenge that required that I be taken out of a private school and homeschooled. I have graduated high school, and as I write this book, will start college in a few days. I learned how to conquer the seemingly unconquerable and I want to share my wisdom with others so they too can overcome any obstacle that stops them. My challenges were difficult, so difficult in fact, that I wouldn't have been able to complete them without smaller goals. I had to be cautious, at times though because I would get so happy about achieving a smaller goal that I didn't want to keep waiting and working for the larger one. I had to learn that the end reward was worth waiting for and more valuable than the short-term reward. Long- term thinking is the key to success in life. Goals must be waited and worked for in order for them to pay off big. If I choose to think short term, I will see some small rewards. However, we will never know what our true potential is if we don't create long term goals. Prosperity, fitness, intelligence and spirituality don't just develop overnight. It takes time and effort to make those things possible. *"With man this is impossible, but with God ALL things are possible."* (Matthew 19:26)

Everything I do and every decision I make is a long or short-term choice. What I decide to do today will impact tomorrow. Short-term thinking is simply viewing the consequences of a given action only briefly. Concerning myself with only the short term can easily be my downfall. There are so many examples proving this is true that many books on the topic could be filled. I have also seen so many examples of out-of the box thinking such as Ronald Reagan, Pope John Paul II, Steve Jobs, and Mother Teresa. These people and many others saw what the future could hold and acted on it. Innovative thinking combined with matching actions equals a success beyond measure. *"For I know the plans I have for you,"* declares the LORD, *"plans to prosper you and not to harm you, plans to give you hope and a future."* (Jeremiah 29:11)

So what is success? The answer to that question varies with everybody. Personally, I believe that success is obtained through a balanced life achieved by following God's principles. These principles are the tools that we need to obtain a success and that can impact the lives of many. If these principles are applied in addition to the concept of long-term thinking and hard work, then success will be achieved because my life, destined by God, will be fulfilled. *"Have no fear of moving into the unknown. Simply step out fearlessly knowing that I am with you, therefore no harm can befall you; all is very, very well. Do this in complete faith and confidence."* (Pope John Paul II)

My sister and I playing a duet

Chapter 1 - Flexing Your Muscles
When Facing a Crisis

Looking back into the history of my life, I see all the storms of my challenges with their tracks. I see how those storms have been decimated with the sun coming out. While in those storms, it seemed like they would never go away and that the sun would never shine again. As a teenager looking back on my past, I am so glad that I didn't give up when I wanted to. I'm glad that I fought the hurricanes with their fierce winds and sharp projectiles. I am glad that I never gave up on the game of life.

My challenges started early in life when I was two months old in the womb. I had a stroke in-utero (also known as a mild form of Cerebral Palsy) that weakened my right side, similar to a stroke experienced by older people. One of the visible side affects was my weakened right hand that it couldn't open and remained in a tightly clenched fist. My hand was so tight in fact, that it wasn't until three months after my birth that it was pried open finger by finger. My occupational therapist showed my parents how to open my hand by turning my right wrist down which loosened my fingers.

It was a bit confusing for my parents seeing that my hand had no function whatsoever. When I played with toys, I would just use my left hand leaving my other one clenched tight at my chest. When I crawled, I used my elbows and forearms to drag my body behind me, which were not normal physical movements of a baby.

Immediately after my birth, the doctors set out to find what was wrong with me. When I was about six months old, a pediatric neurologist ordered an MRI, with the intent to discover the reason for my weakened right side. When the results came back, he showed my parents the images of my brain indicating scar tissue on the left side- as a result of the stroke. My parents asked what that would mean for me when I got older and the neurologist said: "Well, George won't be able to do some things. For instance, he will not be able to play the piano or baseball."

Sitting in the doctor's office hearing those words was probably a bit shocking for my parents. My parents could have been very discouraged by the news from the neurologist that I had a stroke, but they didn't let it stop me from learning to play the piano. They believed that the Lord would help me overcome my challenges.

Since my mother was a piano teacher, she knew the use of my right hand on the keys would be good occupational therapy. I started playing by pressing each right hand finger one-by-one on the keys to strengthen them since my fingers were so weak. This greatly upset me and at times I wanted to quit. "What's the use learning to play the piano when I'm not strong enough to play it!" I would scream. My mom saw my distress and at times considered letting me quit but deep down in her heart, she realized that playing the piano was the best thing for me. For a while, I was mad at her for forcing me to continue but I had no choice but to obey. It was a good thing too because over the years, my right hand fingers became stronger, and I was able to play piano pieces at the same level as my friends. I compensated for more difficult pieces by crossing hands to complete difficult chords. Later, I was able to play chords with my right hand, but not after much time consuming practice.

As a result of my daily practice, which seemed futile at times, my right hand got stronger, and I won awards at the University of Louisiana. It was then that I looked back at all my practicing and realized that it was useful for my hand, as well as my brain. "Scientists say that children who are exposed to music, or those who play an instrument, do better in school than those who don't especially in math and science. Recent research suggests that exposure to music may benefit a child's reading age, IQ and the development of certain parts of the brain."

One benefit of playing the piano was not readily recognized. When playing certain songs that required the damper pedal, my mother insisted on me using my right foot. This was difficult since my right foot was also very weak. I argued and complained that there really was no point in using my foot but my mother would not give in. One particular day when I was upset about using my right foot, we had to go to the physical therapist for a checkup. The therapist noticed I was not my usual happy self and asked what was wrong. I explained how my mother insisted I use my right foot for the piano pedal. The therapist sided with me, stating that I should use the foot that is easier. To my surprise, my mother, who is generally non-argumentative, did not back down. My mother looked at the therapist in the eye and said, "George will someday drive and I want him to use his right foot." Both the therapist and I lost that day but in the long run, I won. Today, I am able to drive confidently and comfortably with my strong, right foot on the pedal as a result of my mom's decision.

It is interesting to note that playing an instrument can greatly enlarge the cerebral cortex with a concert pianist having a cerebral cortex on average 30% larger than an intellectual who didn't play an instrument. I can use the fact that instruments can increase the size of the cerebral to my advantage. The cerebral cortex is responsible for a wide variety of things including communications and abstract thinking. As the result of the development of those areas of the brain due to piano, I now have a greater potential to be successful in different areas of life involving those parts of my brain. In fact, a CA study found that 75% of CEO's in Silicon Valley had musical instrument lessons when they were younger.

It's important for me to say that I couldn't have done it without help, encouragement, and lots of prayers. In fact, I would have probably stopped a long time ago if it weren't for other people cheering me on. The things I had to face were so challenging, and I needed constant support from others to stay motivated. It didn't happen quickly, but I was able to overcome many challenges in my life, and you can overcome your challenges as well. Considering my daily struggles, I think the main essentials to our success are: a strong willpower, the help of friends, parents, God and a good work ethic.

Not only did I have physical weaknesses, I also had severe health problems, which were cured as a result of my strong supportive family and my determination to be strong.

One of my health problems, severe asthma, started early in life and lasted until I was 7 years old. The asthma attacks happened often during the day and the only treatment that worked was a nebulizer with a medication called Albuterol (a strong steroid) that allowed me to breathe. Steroids, while never healthy, were my only option. My parents knew that I couldn't stay on the steroids but then again it was our only option and we had to accept that fact. Around midnight, I would wake up wheezing so badly that I was unable to go back to sleep. I was afraid, and I felt like I was suffocating. To help me breathe, my dad would comfort me at night and bring in the nebulizer for regular treatments. This happened night after night for years. At times, the nebulizer did not work and we would end up in the ER where I was nearly blue from lack of oxygen. These asthma attacks also occurred when we traveled by plane making trips difficult. Our first stop when landing would frequently be the ER.

In addition to asthma, I also had numerous ear infections. These infections were so bad that I would have to go to the doctor's office every week for antibiotics. The pain was so intense that I would cry hysterically.

One Christmas Eve, the infection was so severe and my temperature had risen so quickly that we went to the ER. While I was there, I had several seizures and the doctor sent me by ambulance 30 miles away to the Children's Hospital of Philadelphia (CHOP) for a spinal tap and further tests. We celebrated Christmas Day that year in the hospital and again when we returned home a couple of days later. On Christmas Day, a motorist group came and handed out presents to all the children at the hospital. My face glowed with pleasure as I received a giant teddy bear that I could snuggle with at night. The presents they handed out were even better than the ones I got at home and what was even greater was that I had twice as many presents. Though my Christmas was made much more pleasant that year, my doctor visits weren't very enjoyable. I would have to lie still on a mat while the doctors checked out my ears or sinuses.

These health issues, in addition to my weakened right side, added to the worries of my parents. However, their concern did not stop them from seeing my true potential. My parents saw how my struggles got me down. My weakened right side irritated me. I couldn't play with my toys because of my right hand. For example, as I carried my toy cast-iron tractor with my left hand, the tractor would slip out of my hand and drop on my toes, causing much pain. In addition, I couldn't carry books or toys with my right hand because it wasn't strong. I had trouble eating because I could only use my left hand, which caused me to spill food all over myself. At times, I wouldn't even want to carry my own toys or feed myself, because I didn't want to hurt or spill on myself.

As I faced physical and health challenges, I became fearful at times. I eventually learned that fear would paralyze me and stop me from reaching goals that seemed unattainable. I was afraid of bicycling, swimming, and jogging, for example since it was hard physically. Because of that fear, I didn't attempt to conquer those challenges until I was older. When I became fearful, I would often overreact to a challenge causing me to fail. My parents regularly quote this Bible verse to me and my sisters to overcome fear: *"God did not give me a spirit of fear, but of power, and of love and of a sound mind."* (2 Timothy 1:7)

In addition to quoting verses, I use visualization to fight fear. In my mind, I visualize myself not being afraid, and it really helps. I learned this technique from reading a book about President Theodore Roosevelt who was afraid of public speaking among other things. Roosevelt would pretend to not be afraid of public speaking, and then he was able to successfully give a speech. He had to use visualization to pretend not to be afraid, and through this technique, Roosevelt conquered the fear of public speaking. *"Let arms give place to the robe, and the laurel of the warriors yield to the tongue of the orator."* (Cicero)

Fighting fear at all times will help anyone accomplish his or her goals. I had to conquer the fear of making mistakes and realize that it's all right if there are mistakes. Mistakes are part of life and they come with tackling challenges. I've made a lot of mistakes, and I know I will make more, but I try to learn from each one and use that knowledge for the next attempt. *"We must not say every mistake is a foolish one."* (Cicero)

A great historical example of a person who made tons of mistakes was Thomas Edison. Edison tried over 3,000 different substances to make the filament of a light bulb until he finally found one that lasted long enough to make the light bulb cheap enough to sell and make money. Edison looked at all those attempts as ways how **not** to make a light bulb, he never saw it as 3,000 failures and that's why he finally succeeded. *"There are no negatives in life, only challenges to overcome that will make you stronger."* (Eric Bates, reporter and author)

My parents could have been fearful about my asthma and ear infections. They could have stopped trying when the doctors did not have answers to my health issues. Instead, they prayed for wisdom, and God guided them to nutritional changes in my diet. *"The only thing we have to fear is fear itself."* (Franklin Roosevelt)

If my parents had been fearful, then I would not be where I am today. It is good to get advice from doctors and professionals, but my parents and I relied mainly on God's infinite wisdom for my healing and future. This verse has given me hope when my future, at times, seemed hopeless: *"Nothing is impossible with God."* (Luke 1:37)

Learning to be comfortable playing in front of others

Chapter 2 - Igniting the Internal Engine

Nutrition played an important role in my strength, mentally and physically. A good diet seems like a basic concept, although it was a challenge for me. It was also a struggle for my parents to promote good nutrition, because I had tantrums. The food texture was fearful for me. I later learned that I had sensory issues relating to the textures of food, which caused me to cry and scream. Nutritious food, such as spinach, broccoli, and protein had unusual textures that frightened me and felt strange on my taste buds. My parents read a statistic that it takes over 70 times of eating a particular food for taste buds to get used to the texture. I conquered the fear of food thus providing me with a strong muscular body able to compete in a mini-triathlon. In addition, proper nutrition helped me soar in school where I graduated early into college with a 4.0 and full tuition paid.

The nutrition relation was seen early on in my life. While most boy toddlers spent their days playing with building blocks, I was moody and unable to focus long on playing with toys or looking at books. Changes were seen in a stronger focus after my parents worked with me to eat nutritiously. I started to enjoy learning. I was able to focus on reading, building Lego castles, and started drawing intricate pictures. In addition, in grade school, I began reading at a college level due in part, I believe, to good nutrition. Early in my life, I saw a connection between nutrition and brain function. I also started feeling better physically.

According to Rose Erickson's article, *How Nutrition Affects the Brain of Adolescents*: "Nutrition has a strong impact on the brain of an adolescent. A healthy, nutritious diet can improve brain function, boosting your child's performance both in and out of school. However, a poor diet can cause serious disturbances to the brain, affecting all of your child's bodily and mental function."

Nutrition proved to be an important factor in my life. Perhaps my story of struggling with food will help others overcome trials and give encouragement to parents and children to eat healthy. Following is just a short scenario of my battle to overcome my fear of food.

When I was a baby, I was somewhat spoiled, because I got whatever I cried for. There was no discipline initially as I was the first child of my parents and on top of that, I had physical and health challenges so my parents were hesitant to discipline me. My mother thought that when babies cried for milk, they should get it. That is the case for most babies, but I was not like most babies. As a baby, I cried for milk constantly, because it comforted me. I drank almost a gallon a day, and after quickly gaining too much weight, the doctors put me on a diet restricting my milk intake.

Several years down the road, my diet got worse. My meals consisted of: applesauce, yogurt, macaroni, goldfish crackers, and milk. While applesauce and yogurt are good, my diet was not balanced. I did not want to eat vegetables, protein, or many types of fruit. I refused to give up my select foods for the more nutritious meals my mother offered. Smooth textures were just to appealing to my palate.

If anything described my attitude, it was stubborn. I was a strong-willed child. My mom tried all sorts of things including leaving the food in front of me and then taking it away when I wouldn't eat. I would scream and hide under a chair hoping that I wouldn't have to eat the greens. At one point, I went without eating for three days. A diet of no vegetables, protein, and little fruit took its toll on my mood as well as my health.

According to Erickson: "Nutrition affects the way an adolescent's brain handles mood. Processed foods, prepackage baked goods, candy and other sugary foods can quickly raise the sugar levels in the blood stream. In retaliation, the brain signals the release of insulin, a hormone that helps sugar enter the cells of the body. When there is too much sugar in the blood, the insulin cannot do its job properly and the blood sugar level dips. As a result, a child can feel moody, angry and agitated. Simple sugars found in complex carbohydrates are best for the brain. They provide time-released energy rather than a sudden sugar spike."

My health was also deteriorating with numerous ear infections and increased severe asthma. In the case of my sinus infections, it is very likely that I had developed an allergy to milk given the large quantity of milk I drank a day. According to an article on *livestrong.com*: "Andorra Pediatrics states that research proves that milk does not increase mucus production. If you're allergic to dairy products, you can experience increased mucus production and congestion in the sinus cavity, which can lead to a sinus infection." My parents realized a change in diet was necessary for me to regain my health.

One doctor is making a direct connection between asthma and eating. Colleen Pierre, R.D. documents Dr. Shane Broughton, Ph.D. in her article *The Anti-Asthma Diet*: "Unlike most researchers who study asthma, Dr. Broughton isn't focused on dust mites, pollen, or pollution. 'Many people believe contaminants are to blame for the drastic increase in asthma rates, but my studies suggest it has much more to do with what we're feeding children," he says, 'Diet is key'.

The notion that potato chips may be more problematic than pollution, and desserts more devilish than dust mites, seems suspect until you realize that Dr. Broughton isn't the only researcher who attributes escalating asthma rates at least in part to dismal diets. In the United Kingdom, Ireland, New Zealand, and Australia -- countries where asthma now affects 30% of kids and is still climbing -- the link between the disease and diet has been studied by leading scientists for more than decade."

After much prayer, my parents came to the conclusion that I would only get stronger and healthier with a nutritious diet. If not, my situation would only get worse with me having future possible health issues. Some of these issues, according to an article on *fitday.com* are:

- Decreased energy
- Poor performance and obesity
- Damage to the heart and liver
- Diabetes

After consulting with numerous experts who were at a loss as to how to handle my eating tantrums, my parents prayed for a plan. This plan evolved from God's wisdom and the example of a priest. My parents relied heavily on the verse in James about *"praying for wisdom and God will pour it out abundantly"*. My parent's determination to mold my eating habits was influenced by a family friend, a priest who came to dinner frequently. My mother would ask him what his favorite meal was and his standard response was, "I am thankful for any food placed in front of me." This priest said his mother always wanted him to eat whatever was served to him so he would not insult any families or cultures if he would be a missionary.

This example inspired a new rule involving me to take three bites of whatever the family was eating, and then I would be able to eat whatever I wanted. At first, it seemed like this wouldn't work but as time went on I learned what was expected. I knew that, if I gulped those three bites down, then I was free to eat whatever I wanted. After I successfully began to eat three bites, my mom gradually upped the requirements. I progressed steadily until the moment of truth came – a formal farewell dinner prepared for us by neighbors in Philadelphia who were sad we were moving to Louisiana.

My father's job offer in Louisiana meant that we were going to move from our close-knit neighborhood in Philadelphia. When our Italian neighbors learned of the move, they invited us to an authentic Italian dinner as a going away present. The meal (for those with good eating habits) promised to be tasty, with an array of authentic Italian dishes. My parents looked forward to the meal but were concerned about how I would react. I was eating fine at home but this was the first time I would be tested in public.

Prior to the festive meal, my parents instructed me to eat whatever they gave me and have a gracious attitude. My mother told me not to be dishonest and say, "I like the meal" when I didn't like it, however, I should say, "Thank you for your hard work cooking." As a reward, I would get my favorite food when I got home.

Many neighbors were seated at the long table when we arrived. We sat down at the table decorated in its finest décor -flowers in vases with Italian artwork painted on them and the china bowls complete with shiny silverware. Gold plated spoons sat in bowls, which were soon to hold the scrumptious dishes.

The cooks came out carrying their masterpieces covered in linen cloths and set them before us. I took the lid off of the one nearest to me and found to my absolute horror a dark gooey, green substance, which looked somewhat like spinach. Nevertheless, I had to have a little bit on my plate.

Our hosts watched with expectation as I took the first bite. The taste was absolutely repulsing and I gagged. Nevertheless, I smiled and said, "Thank you very much."

The hosts were delighted and exclaimed, "Look! George likes it!"

My parents were very happy about my good table manners and hugged me close. I received my reward, and got invited to more dinner parties.

The importance of learning to eat a wide variety of foods can't be more emphasized for health and mental reasons as well as social situations. We never know when we will be traveling and our tolerance will be required.

I am fortunate that my parents started me on a healthy diet early because, if they didn't, I would have had a harder time mastering it when I was older. Today, I don't have to worry about hurting someone else's feelings by rejecting their food. I eat a wide range of food even though there are a couple things like bean sprouts, which I'm still not too wild about. The discipline of eating healthy helped me feel better. After adding more vegetables and fruit, my ear infections cleared up almost immediately. One doctor couldn't believe it and asked my parents what they did to cure me. Of course, prayer is the number one answer and I thank God for my healing.

The next healing happened about a year later when my asthma was totally cured. I went from wheezing and coughing with nightly nebulizer treatments to being able to breath freely. Good nutrition not only helped me feel better, but also improved my overall physical appearance.

Studies have indicated the connection between food and health. According to an article by Diane Lynn on *www.lifestrong.com*: "The food you consume impacts more than how much you weigh, but also affects your energy levels, digestive function, risk for diseases and other bodily functions... you need at least 2 1/2 cups of vegetables and 2 cups of fruits each day, according to the *U.S. Dietary Guidelines.* However, the *Centers for Disease Control and Prevention* indicates that only one-third of adults eat more than two servings of fruit a day, and slightly more than one-fourth eat more than three servings of vegetables a day, as of 2009."

Fast food restaurants are popular and a temptation to many teenagers including me. Between the years 1970 and 2001, fast food restaurants increased from 30,000 to 220,000 in number. According to *Ohio Medical Group*, "Due to the fast food culture, about 60% of Americans are overweight or obese. Obesity has many health risks including:

- Coronary Heart disease
- Stroke
- Hypertension
- Diabetes
- Cancer
- Gall Bladder disease
- Osteoarthritis
- Respiratory problems

"Let food be your medicine and medicine be your food." (Hippocrates)

Obesity shouldn't be a problem for us teenagers due to our high metabolisms. However, more and more teens nowadays find themselves on couches playing video games and eating junk food. Not surprisingly, the percentage of obese teens in 2008 had risen from 5% in 1980 to 18%. With advancements in technology, came a more sedentary lifestyle in teens and adults alike.

A good way we can combat obesity is by managing our diet. I consider my body like a Ferrari. If I want it to run well, I need to give my body the right kind of fuel and maintain it. If I eat high-end food, then my performance will be high end. Is a Dr. Pepper soda with 250 calories, forty grams of sugar and five grams of protein low or high-octane fuel? How about a protein smoothie with 400 calories, twenty grams of sugar and twenty grams of protein? This drink has more calories but it has less carbs and more protein.

Eating healthy and working out has boosted my confidence. I am no longer weak physically or mentally, and I have conquered my fear for food. I like being perceived as a muscular young man full of energy for life and successful at my studies. The realization of my body *"being a temple of the Holy Spirit"* (1 Corinthians 3:16) encourages me to take great care of the food and liquids I consume, so I can remain healthy and in peak performance.

George practicing his speaking skills at a poetry recitation event

George doing backstroke at a swim tournament

Chapter 3 - Witness Physical Fitness

As my nutrition improved, so did my physical strength. Initially, I wasn't strong in nutrition or physical fitness. I did obtain a better immune system from healthy eating but continued struggling with the physical aspect especially my weakened right arm, hand, leg, and foot. Aside from dance classes two times a week, I didn't do any other activity. Music was a motivating factor in dance and other activities but I needed more exercise as I was sadly out of shape. My limited physical exercise became apparent by my physical therapist who noticed minimal exercises exhausted me. Since my physical therapist was an avid jogger, he suggested I start with a daily regime of jogging to build my cardiovascular strength. Jogging was the beginning of a more intense exercise regime. I later added swimming and cycling both extremely difficult with a weak leg and arm. Through struggling to jog, swim, and cycle, my parents reminded me that: *"I can do all things through Christ who strengthens me."* (Philippians 4:13)

My physical therapist's suggestion to jog didn't sound like fun. However, my mother thought jogging was a good idea and began a daily running routine as our new P.E. We started slowly but to me it seemed like a marathon. Our route started with jogging to the neighbor's house next door. After I was able to complete that course without falling over, we extended it to the end of the street, which is maybe 500 feet! The runs seemed torturous and usually ended with me crying. Man was I out of shape! My mother would try to motivate me with mental images to conquer heat like skiing or when it was cold, she would tell me to pretend I was sweating on a hot summer day at the beach. Sometimes it worked, but mainly I was just so out of shape that I was miserable. However, after much persistence and a daily running routine, I was able to complete the small runs and later graduated to longer ones entailing a mile and then two miles. I couldn't believe I was actually enjoying running and started to ask to run even more.

Recently, I participated in a triathlon that consisted of a two hundred meter swim, five-mile bike and two mile run. It is interesting to note that I completed the run in fourteen minutes, an average of seven minutes per mile. Without prayer and persistence, I would never have dreamed I could jog that far let alone jog that fast.

Exercising can be beneficial in many ways. According to an article on *nutristadtegy.com*, exercise.

- Reduces the risk of dying prematurely.
- Reduces the risk of dying prematurely from heart disease.
- Reduces the risk of developing diabetes.
- Reduces the risk of developing high blood pressure.
- Helps reduce blood pressure in people who already have high blood pressure.
- Reduces the risk of developing colon cancer.
- Reduces feelings of depression and anxiety.
- Helps control weight.
- Helps build and maintain healthy bones, muscles, and joints.
- Helps older adults become stronger and better able to move about without falling.
- Promotes psychological well being.

The *U.S. Department of Health and Human Services* recommends that young people aged 6–17 years participate in at least 60 minutes of physical activity daily."

The *Center for Disease Control and Prevention* (CDC) notes that inactivity causes serious health problems: "Overweight and obesity, which are influenced by physical inactivity and poor diet, can increase one's risk for diabetes, high blood pressure, high cholesterol, asthma, arthritis, and poor health status. Physical inactivity increases one's risk for dying prematurely, dying of heart disease, and developing diabetes, colon cancer, and high blood pressure."

I am very grateful to my physical therapist for his suggestion that I should start jogging, even though I was upset and pouted for weeks after. My physical therapist did his job and that encouragement helped me to get stronger.

Many examples of athletes overcoming trials have influenced me to keep going in spite of my physical weaknesses. One such example is

Joe Decker, the fittest man in the world, who ran in extreme races such as a 135-mile desert run and an adventure race of 520 miles across the Himalaya Mountains. Joe showed me that it doesn't matter whether we are fat or thin; we all have the ability to exercise. As a kid, Decker was chubby and got even larger after a football injury. After attempting a college education, he dropped out and became a bartender. Decker partied, drinking and eating, eventually becoming even more out of shape. Embarrassed by his large stomach, Decker would wear an oversized shirt when swimming. At times, Decker was so depressed that he contemplated suicide. Realizing the implications of these thoughts, he returned home to rest and recover. Decker did not give up. With an old weight set and by walking, he increased his fitness level to a point where he could run a 5K and eventually extreme races of 35 miles and 520 miles.

Decker wasn't cut out to be the world's fittest man from the start. He started small and worked his way up. Decker inspired me to start small when it came to jogging – first a 15-minute walk with a 5 minute jog. Later, I was able to run with ease. I worked up to a 20 minute jog, then 30 until reaching an hour.

Although I have never run a marathon, I have felt the pains that come with working toward a goal and the feeling of victory that comes with accomplishing one. Pain and victory were especially obvious when I learned how to swim.

When my family moved to Louisiana over ten years ago, my parents decided that it would be a good idea to have a pool at the new house to help strengthen my right leg and arm.

Swimming was extremely difficult for me since my entire right side was weak and swimming requires coordination on both sides of the body. My parents had me in swim lessons since I was a baby, but I would fuss when no one was holding on to me. When we moved to our home in Louisiana, I was about four years old. The pool terrified me. When I did get in the pool, I had to have arm floaters and someone in the pool with me at all times.

My parents prayed I would be brave enough to get in the pool with a swim vest and not require an adult to hold onto me. They thought additional private lessons would help. The teacher was very patient and helpful. *"Patience is bitter, but its fruit is sweet.* (Aristotle) After three months of lessons, she told my parents that I could float for about a minute, but the weakness in my leg and arm continued to make it difficult to swim. When doing swimming freestyle for example, I would swim crookedly because my left arm was rotating faster and with more force than my right arm. My swim teacher told my parents it would be about three years before I could swim.

My parents were not discouraged. They prayed and fasted that I would not be afraid. While in the pool they would sing to me, *"I can do all things through Christ who strengthens me."* (Philippians 4:13)

Although I had a wonderful swim teacher, her prediction was wrong. Three months, after my teacher said I wouldn't be able to swim for three years, a miracle happened. It was Father's day, and my dad and sister decided to take a swim in the pool. I sat on the side, dangling my feet in the water without a swim vest, because I didn't plan on swimming. I asked the Holy Spirit to take away my fears and suddenly felt empowered. I knew I could swim. My dad was shocked to see me swimming across the pool without a floating device or help from anyone. Even though swimming was difficult because of my asymmetry, I worked hard at it, and I was able to swim like a fish.

Later, at the age of twelve, I joined a swim team of COLA (City of Lafayette Aquatics). While I knew how to swim, this was as a totally different challenge. My instructor Coach Sarah Landreneau pushed me to use my right arm to rotate for the backstroke and butterfly. Coach Sarah didn't go easy on my as she encouraged me to kick my right leg which strengthened the muscle. This was very difficult and I felt exhausted after every practice. Another extreme challenge for me was diving off the four-foot high diving board. Standing on the ledge looking into the water sometimes made my stomach sick with fear, but I pushed on and overcame this fear. My parents encouraged me with this verse, *"God did not give me a spirit of fear but of power and of love and of a sound mind."* (2 Timothy 1:7)

After much work, I completed the fifty-meter freestyle in a minute and twenty five seconds. My speed was very disappointing though given the fact that the ten year olds had better scores than me, a twelve year old. Even at practice, the younger swimmers would pass me as if I was like a manatee, and they were graceful, dolphins. My right hand and foot would create drag while my left arm easily moved through the water. I was so slow, in fact that the team would start another exercise before I finished the previous one. After completing the exercise, I had to immediately start on the next one with little or no break. There were many times I wanted to quit and I felt defeated. I looked around at the other swimmers with strong arms and legs and then looked at my weak, small right arm and weak leg and felt jealous, even sad. I wondered why God made me this way, but then I heard my parents encouraging words echoing in my mind "George, *'you are fearfully and wonderfully made'* in God's image and God has huge plans for you.*"* (Psalm 139:14) This gave me the strength to push on. I knew that, if I pushed myself, I would get stronger.

My swim practices would last for up to two hours, twice a week. I was so exhausted afterward that I would return home, eat supper, and go to bed. The following day, I would wake with a sore hand and leg wondering if my swimming was helping or hurting me. In addition, I didn't see my lap time decrease.

A year later, I noticed my speed increasing at practice Finally, after a fifty meter race, I looked up at the scoreboard and saw that my time was forty-five seconds. I had cut 40 seconds off my time! At that point, I recognized just how far I had come in a short time. I was transforming from a walrus into swift dolphin.

In an article, *Fitness Basics: Swimming is for Everyone,* by Barbara Russi Samataro "Exercise physiologist Robert A. Robergs says swimming is a good fitness choice for just about everyone, especially those who have physical limitations or who find other forms of exercise painful. 'It is a good, whole-body exercise that has low impact for people with arthritis, musculoskeletal, or weight limitations,' says Robergs, director of the exercise physiology laboratories at The University of New Mexico in Albuquerque. Water's buoyancy accommodates the unfit as well as the fit. Water cushions stiff joints or fragile bones that might be injured by the impact of land exercises. When immersed to the waist, your body bears just 50% of its weight; immersed to the chest, it's 25%-35%; and to the neck, 10%. 'Swimming is also desirable for people with exercise-induced asthma,' says Robergs, 'as the warm, humid air [around the pool] causes less irritation to the airways."

According to Tay Stratton, head swim coach at the Little Rock Athletic Club, 'swimming engages all the major muscle groups, including the shoulders, back, abdominals, legs, hips, and glutes,' she says. 'And because water affords 12 times the resistance as air in every direction.'"

My parents tell me how I helped them appreciate ordinary activities like jogging, swimming, and even bicycling, all exercises that come easy to most people. For me, bicycling was a particularly challenging exercise.

I got my first bicycle at the age of four. The bike had training wheels to keep me from tipping over but they didn't help much. My right foot would slip off the pedals due to having weak muscles from Cerebral Palsy. My dad fixed the problem by getting pedal clips used by avid bicycle racers. This solved the foot problem. Next, I had trouble steering the handles due to my weakened right hand, which, much to my frustration, couldn't keep. I would nearly run into trees because I couldn't control the handles. With a parent on either side of the bike guiding me, I was able to mainly use my left hand for steering. Biking was work but a bit enjoyable until about the first grade when all my neighborhood friends began taking their training wheels off. Without training wheels, I felt like I could not control steering, pedals, and balance with a body that didn't have symmetry on both sides.

I may have just avoided biking altogether but my parents knew how to get me to do things and that was with money. They offered me twenty dollars if I would learn to ride a bike. I loved the prospect of earning a few dollars but was less than thrilled about the hard work involved. Still, it was part of the deal, so I began working on my biking during lunch breaks with my dad when most kids were at school. I was 10 years old and I didn't want anyone my age seeing me unable to ride a bicycle. I watched the neighborhood children my age and younger ride their bikes with ease. They had symmetry with two strong legs, feet, and arms. I looked at my weak, small right leg and weak right arm and wondered if I could every ride a bike. My parents words continued to ring through my ears, *"George, you can do all things through Christ who strengthens you. That means ALL things not some things."* (Philippians 4:13) This gave me the courage to keep trying.

My dad worked with me day-after day, running up and down the sidewalk with me letting go briefly to see if I could balance myself. I almost gave up until one day I heard a message at mass about the power of small David conquering the giant Goliath. After mass, my mother turned to me and said, "George, your bicycle is your Goliath." I then asked my mom, "Do you think I can conquer it today?" She confidently answered, "Today is the day."

Immediately, we went home and tried again on the bike. After the third try, I rode down the street, without my mother holding onto my bike. I shouted to my mother, "Hey mom, it was the third try that I conquered my bike – the Goliath. Do you know what the number three is?" She said, "What, George?" I replied, "The number three stands for the Trinity."

I had conquered my bike – my Goliath but only after I had worked for many years going up and down the sidewalk with my parents. Praying and visualizing myself jogging, swimming, and bicycling helped me reach those goals. I continue visualizing for success in other activities such as weightlifting.

When I began to lift weights about two and a half years ago, I started out light and basic. I made tons of mistakes like having bad form and overcompensating with my left side because of my weaker right side and my gains were lopsided as a result. Fortunately, there were many people at the gym who knew what they were doing. I consulted a personal trainer, Travis Tolbert at City Club's fitness center. Travis had me do unique exercises and gave me great advice to get stronger. Travis had a focus on kinesiology to provide a workout program that was completely foreign to me. "Kinesiology, derived from the Greek words kinesis (movement) and kinein (to move), also known as human kinetics, is the science of human movement. It is a discipline that focuses on physical activity. "Kinesiology addresses physiological, mechanical, and psychological mechanisms. Applications of kinesiology to human health include: biomechanics and orthopedics, strength & conditioning, sport psychology, rehabilitation, such as physical and occupational therapy, as well as sport and exercise."

My personal trainer, Travis, showed me an entirely new approach to strengthening my right hand and leg. It was difficult but I had the desire to be strong so I continued with his workouts, involving exercise bands, balance, and good form. "Muscle testing used by kinesiologists does not measure the pure physical strength that a muscle can produce, but rather how the nervous system controls its muscle functions. There are over two hundred bones connected to hundreds of muscles in the body. These all need to be working properly together, to enable good nerve, lymph and blood supply throughout the body. Gentle corrections and alignment of these systems may be applied to balance the body's physical structure."

Travis helped me realize that my asymmetry could bring severe consequences to my health in the future such as back misalignment, arthritis, and posture. According to an article from *Mark's Daily Apple.com*, muscular asymmetry can cause many physical problems including lordosis (an abnormal inward curve of the spine attributed to weak hamstrings) as well as an undesirable cosmetic appearance of tiny legs and giant upper body for example. In my instance, I would have a giant left leg and arm, and a small right leg and arm. This was far from appealing and I worked hard to prevent that making great gains on my right side in the progress. At first, the gains were primarily on my left side but as time went on and I learned the proper techniques and my gains began to shift. Today, my gains are much more proportional if not downright in favor of my right side, and I am friends with many people at the gym including six other helpful personal trainers. I couldn't have made much progress without the help of Travis and the other personal trainers including Jacob Azenne and Nate Pry.

In the case of my progress for a stronger hand and leg, my level of fitness impeded me when I was young but today, the strength of my right hand, leg and stamina are much better enabling me to carry heavier objects and be more productive. I do not think of my body as broken or weak, I look at my body as the temple of God; a body to be respected and well cared for. *"Or do you not know that your body is a temple of the Holy Spirit within you, whom you have from God? You are not your own, for you were bought with a price. So glorify God in your body."* (1 Corinthians 6:19-20)

"God did not give me a spirit of fear, but of power, and of love, and of a sound mind." -2 Timothy 1:7

My sisters are my cheerleaders

Chapter 4 - Control Attraction
To Electronic Distraction

My parents always quoted this Bible verse in terms of the books I read and the videos and television shows I watched-- *"As you think, so you shall be"* (Proverbs 23:7). I believe that whatever is in our minds will mold us into the people we will become. For example, when I was younger, I watched an episode of *Ninja Turtles* and then began acting out by kicking others. My mother recognized where the actions came from and did not let me watch it again.

Negative values can translate into negative feelings and negative feelings into negative actions. For me, it was a visible chain effect!

My parents guarded my mental, physical and personal health by limiting electronic devices, especially in the way of gaming devices. Some games contain much violence such as *Call of Duty*, *Blue Angels* and *Grand Auto Theft* to name a few. While other games aren't terrible, like *Mario Cart*, games like *Call of Duty* are called into question. According to a study done by Craig Bushman & Brad Anderson, physiologists at Iowa State University, after a given amount of time playing violent videogames, participants can automatically prime aggressive thoughts.

While watching *Call of Duty* once, I saw captured soldiers being executed by the gamers. Recently, a teenage video gamer killed a twelve-year-old girl. The mother of the teen turned him in after the fact but perhaps the killing could have been prevented if her son was not playing violent games. I believe that there may be a connection.

According to an article on the website *Medical News Today:* "The annual meeting of the Radiological Society of North America (RSNA) was presented with a study made of the brain of young men, using fMRI scans (functional magnetic resonance imaging). In as little as one week, regions of the brain associated with cognitive function and emotional control had noticeable changes. What the researchers did was take 22 healthy adult males, age 18 to 29, who were not avid game players in the past. The group was split and randomly assigned into two groups of 11. Members of the first group were instructed to play a shooting video game for 10 hours at home for one week and refrain from playing the following week. The second group did not play a violent video game at all during the two-week period. All 22 men were analyzed with an fMRI scan at the beginning of the study and with follow-up exams at one and two weeks. During their examination, the participants also completed an emotional interference task, pressing buttons according to the color of visually presented words. Words indicating violent actions were interspersed among nonviolent action words. In addition, the participants completed a cognitive inhibition counting task. After just one week of playing violent games, the video game group members showed less activation in the left inferior frontal lobe during the emotional task and less activation in the anterior cingulate cortex during the counting task, compared to their baseline results and the results of the control group after one week. After the second week without game play, the changes to the executive regions of the brain were diminished."

Based on a recent study: "Dr. Chou Yuan-hua, at Psychiatry of the Taipei Veterans General Hospital, claims that playing videogames (specifically violent ones) slows blood flow to the brain, and that prolonged exposure can lead to brain damage. Chou's greatest concern seems to be for children, whom he says 'spend far more time [than the 30 minutes of the study] on video games each day, unaware that doing so on a long term basis could damage the frontal lobe of the brain.'" The article ends with a statement from the doctor regarding the physical characteristics of schizophrenia, which happen to be rather similar to those found by his study. Schizophrenia is a mental disorder characterized by a breakdown of thought processes and by poor emotional responsiveness. Common symptoms include:

- Auditory hallucinations
- Paranoid or bizarre delusions,
- Disorganized speech and thinking,
- Significant social or occupational dysfunction.

According to Dr. Choi, there seems to be certain relationships between schizophrenia and gaming."

As mentioned earlier, there are many non-violent, entertaining games that I have enjoyed. Since I tend to be a bit obsessive, I found myself playing for hours and then when I wasn't playing, I found myself thinking about the game. For example, I used to play a game similar to the *Age of Empires*, and I loved it so much that I had a very hard time not thinking about it even though I played the game for about one and a half hours a day. I would get distracted from my studies and chores thinking about how to set up a certain feature or figuring out how to get more clients and expand my empire. I worried that pirates would attack my trading posts and I would plan out all the adjustments to the settlements hours ahead of time. After a while, I realized I was addicted, and I decided to get rid of the game. I quit playing it for good. For some time afterward, I was a bit disappointed and very tempted to resume playing, but I soon forgot about it.

A study released by the Kaiser Family Foundation showed that kids between the ages 8-18 spend an average of seven to thirty-eight hours a week on gaming.

I believe my seemingly mild addiction to this game could have led to a more serious problem. I read, in an article by Kim Carollo "*Man Dies From Blood Clot After Marathon Gaming*" on *ABC News*, the story of a twenty-year-old Englishman who spent up to twelve hours a day gaming. After an entire night of playing on the computer, the man died of a clot thus showing how dangerous gaming can be.

With my obsessive nature, I pray for the *Holy Spirit's fruit of "self-control"* in all areas of my life for balance. My parents also pray for self-control in their own lives as they say they too have an obsessive nature. My dad, a computer programmer, regularly tells us the story of his addiction to a game. My dad was one of the earliest PC programmers starting in 1983. He was excited about the technology and saw computers as the future. While programming software for companies, my dad and his programmer friends would go to the video arcade and play the newest video games of the 80s. My dad's favorite was *Galaga*, where alien rockets shoot space invaders. The game is not 3-D nor does it depict any blood or visual violence. To most, including me, it seems like a game that would not have a negative impact. However, my dad recounts how he played it daily and achieved the high score. He didn't stop at the top. My dad planned and plotted on how he could get an even higher score. He also started going to the video arcade more than once a day. My dad's days were consumed with thoughts of the game and it began to impact his programming. Finally, my dad realized he was addicted to *Galaga*. With this realization, my dad quit the game and was able to focus on his career programming. To date, my dad has two software patents. Perhaps, he wouldn't have achieved those patents, if he had continued to feed his video game addition.

According to an article titled *Kids electronic media use jumps to 53 hours a week* on *USA Today*, the average kid spends 53 hours a week on electronic devices. When I was young, my mother did not know how much time a child should spend on electronic devices and as such let us do quite a bit of electronics. While I was enrolled at the Valley Forge Montessori, the teachers gave my mother specific guidelines on electronics. According to my Montessori teachers, a child should have no more than 3-4 hours of TV and electronics a week. My teachers' guidelines are stricter than the American Academy of Pediatrics. The Academy recommends, "that children over age 2 watch no more than two hours of television per day; younger kids should watch no TV at all. Each hour a kid spends planted in front of the tube is an hour he or she isn't exercising, playing or doing any other constructive activity like reading."

When we lived in the Philadelphia area, my parents considered sending me to the Waldorf Education – where television, computers, and computer games are severely limited and even encouraged to not be kept in the home. According to the Waldorf philosophy, "their central aim is to stimulate the healthy development of the child's own imagination. Waldorf teachers are concerned that electronic media hampers the development of the child's imagination. They are concerned about the physical effects of the medium on the developing child as well as the content of much of the programming. There is more and more research to substantiate these concerns."

Videogames could have become like a huge rock blocking my future path. I was determined to remove this "stumbling block". Video games in addition to TV could have slowed my studies, physical strength, and spiritual growth. I used to enjoy hours of TV until my mother started monitoring my hours and she explained to me that reading would help me get better grades. According to a study by A.C. Nielson Co., Americans watch an average of 34 hours of TV a week. Another study by Nielson revealed that by the time a teen is eighteen, he or she will have seen 200,000 murders on TV. *"If everyone demanded peace instead of another television set, then there'd be peace."* (John Lennon, English musician and songwriter, former member of the Beatles, 1940-1980)

One habit I try to control is eating in front of the television. I tend to eat more even though I am full when watching a television show. I also eat faster when watching an action adventure. Television is a distraction that takes my attention off of what I am eating. According to A.C. Nielson, 66% of the US population watch TV while eating dinner, which may be a contributing factor to the growing obesity population.

In addition to eating more, television impacts my thinking. It is challenging for me to *"hold all thoughts captive to the Lord"* (2 Corinthians 10:5) when barraged with commercials. I have a tendency to want to buy items not needed such as food, cars, clothing, etc. or because a certain tennis shoe will make me run faster. I even start humming commercial jingles that get stuck in my head. Commercials are structured specifically to unlock the door to our emotional side. By doing this, manufacturers have a chance at getting us to buy their products. *"Rich people have small TVs and big libraries, and poor people have small libraries and big TVs."* (Zig Ziglar, American author, salesman, and motivational speaker, 1926-2012)

TV bombards my thoughts by not only trying to sell stuff but also by selling political viewpoints. Politicians use television to appeal to the emotions. In fact, presidents use the television to try and convince people to come to their side of thinking. When the TV was first used in presidential elections, the running candidate for the presidential office who used TV the most defeated his opponent, who didn't use the TV as much by many votes. *"If those in charge of our society - politicians, corporate executives, and owners of press and television - can dominate our ideas, they will be secure in their power."* (Howard Zinn,

American academic historian, playwright, and social activist, 1922-2010)

With my "eye on the future," I am trying to be careful about distractions entering my mind that may steer me away from future goals. I have the authority to control television, video games, and electronics instead of the electronics controlling me. Paul J. Meyer, motivational author, speaker and founder of *Success Motivation International*, warned of such obstacles when encouraging others to reach their goals, *"Crystallize your goals. Make a plan for achieving them and set yourself a deadline. Then with supreme confidence, determination and disregard for obstacles and other people's criticisms carry out your plan."*

My sister, Emily, one year younger was my best PT. She encouraged me to walk.

Chapter 5 - Connect with Wireless Communication

Every time I sit at a computer, I am thankful for the powerful tool sitting on my desk. It's hard to imagine computers didn't exist not too long ago. When my parents were in grade school, they didn't have computers, just typewriters. As I mentioned before, my computer time was limited when I was young but as I got older, my parents allowed me to use the computer more for school and for a few emails to friends. I also was not allowed texting until recently when I got a job. This disappointed me because all of my friends had the ability to text and I felt like the "lone-ranger," the guy many people know but few actually talk to because he is inaccessible. Texting in the case of my job, however, was a plausible reason for my parents to set me up. After setting me up, my parents cautioned me to limit the use of electronic media because it wasn't an appropriate use of my time.

At sixteen, I still do not have a Facebook page even though the majority of my friends have one and don't text nearly as much as my peers. I continued to be confused by my parents' warning not to overuse media. It seems so fun posting photos on Facebook and texting to multiple friends. That was the case until I discovered how accurate my parents were in their statements that electronic media could easily become a waste of time.

"According to A.C. Nielsen, the number of texts being sent is on the rise, especially among teenagers age 13 to 17. The average teenager now sends 3,339 texts per month. There's more, though: teen females send an incredible 4,050 texts per month, while teen males send an average of 2,539 texts. Teens are sending 8% more texts than they were this time last year."

Although I disagreed with my parents early about monitoring my electronics, I have come to appreciate their strictness in this area especially when reading the many dangers that children and teens can encounter.

A study of sites such as Bebo, Facebook and MySpace shows children using them can be at great risk from pedophiles and bullies. More than a quarter of children aged eight to 11 bypass online age restrictions to put reams of intensely personal detail about themselves online. This opens the door to abuse from other people who can manipulate that information and bring them down. A relative of mine became engaged in cyber bullying with another person from school. They would post comments on their Facebook pages and attempt to tear the other person down. Things got so bad that their school principal had them sign a document allowing for the school to kick them out should they continue what they were doing. In the case of cyber bullying, half of teens have fallen prey to cyber bullying with about the same number participating in it, according to the I-SAFE Foundation. Also, more than 25% of teens have been bullied repeatedly through their phones or the Internet, according to the same source.

Growing up, my parents would teach me to think about the words I was about to speak or write so I wouldn't harm another. I would ponder this verse: *"The words of the reckless pierce like swords, but the tongue of the wise brings healing."* (Proverbs 12:18) With my father's profession as a computer programmer, he tells us every word typed into an electronic device can be saved forever on some server. It reminded my of the Bible that *"every word will be accounted for."* (Matthew 12:36)

Communication by electronic media is gaining popularity and is imperative for communication between businesses and family members. Email, texting, Twitter, and Facebook can be very convenient because they help us to keep track of friends and family by sharing information. Unfortunately, these forms of communications in addition to texting can be very distracting and in some instances fatal.

According to an article on *DailyNews.com*: "about 6,000 deaths and a half a million injuries are caused by distracted drivers every year. While teenagers are texting, they spend about 10% of the time outside the driving lane they're supposed to be in. Talking on a cell phone while driving can make a young driver's reaction time as slow as that of a 70-year-old. Answering a text takes away your attention for about five seconds. That is enough time to travel the length of a football field."

For me, Facebook and texting could be a distraction at a critical period in my life when I need to "keep my eye on the future".

I also try to guard my emails and texts to ensure others do not send me anything immodest. According to new research published in the *Archives of Pediatric & Adolescent Medicine* in July 2012: "one-fourth of teens admitted to having sent a sext. And, 76.2% of teens who were asked to send a sext, even if they didn't agree to do it, admitted to having had sexual intercourse, compared to only 38.2% of teens who had not been propositioned." Sexting has consequences including an increased risk of depression. According to an article on *dailyfreepress.com*: "Teenagers who 'sext' are more likely to have symptoms of depression, according to a Newton based Nov. 2 study. 36% of students who had 'sexted' reported depressive symptoms in the past year, according to the study conducted by The Educational Development Center, only 17% of students who have not 'sexted' reported symptoms of depression. The study, which was based on a 2010 survey that included more than 23,000 high school students, also revealed that 13% of high school students who have 'sexted' reported a suicide attempt in the past year, while only 3% of students who had not 'sexted' reported suicide attempts.

With electronics and easy access to the Internet, I try to not put myself into the temptation of immodest images or foul language. I realize that the chances of being exposed to these things are greatly reduced with the introduction of website blockers. For me, they have definitely helped by blocking websites that I wouldn't have even assumed contained bad content.

Website blockers are like rules. I used to think that rules were created to keep me from having fun. I later learned rules gave me freedom from temptation and potential addictions that would have kept me from achieving my goals. Now that I have website blockers installed, I| can use the Internet to its full potential.

Facebook, however, is being used more and more by business to screen potential employers. "A survey commissioned by the online employment website *CareerBuilder* has found that 37% of hiring managers use social networking sites to research job applicants, with over 65% of that group using Facebook as their primary resource.

This data is based on a nationwide survey conducted by *Harris Interactive Researchers* asked more than 2,000 hiring managers and other human resources employees if they use social networking sites to inform hiring decisions and, if so, what kinds of information they looked for and whether or not those findings hurt candidates' chances. Researchers found that 37% of the companies surveyed used social networking sites to prescreen candidates, and 11% said that they planned to start doing so in the future. Only 15% of companies had policies in place that explicitly prohibited human resources department from using the sites as a hiring resource.

Of the hiring managers that looked at social networking sites, 65% reported that they used them to see if the applicant 'presents him- or herself professionally'. Half used the sites to determine if the person would be a good fit with the company's culture, and 45% wanted to learn more about the candidates' qualifications. Twelve percent of hiring managers that use the sites said they were specifically looking for reasons not to hire the person. Nonetheless, 34% of hiring managers said they had come across something that caused them not to hire a candidate. In nearly half of these cases, the person posted a provocative photo or had made reference to drinking or drug use. Other red flags cited were instances in which someone spoke badly about a former employer, lied about their qualifications, or simply were not being able to write well."

I have come to realize that while the Internet can have negative attributes, these can be bypassed with the aid of web blockers, moderation and self-control. Not everything will be blocked, and I will need willpower to avoid the other bad things such as language but web blockers are a definite help. I now have the ability to use the Internet to reach my goals in college and as a professional, in addition to maintaining close relationships with friends and family.

Chapter 6 - Electronic Rise
And Social Demise

My social training began as a toddler. My parents encouraged me to say, "Please" and "Thank-you" when receiving gifts, food, or complements from adults. My parents instructed me to look into people's eyes when talking and answer questions. Social training in my home was an everyday endeavor and continued into all outings. After riding on the train at the zoo, my parents taught me to shake the conductor's hand and thank him. My parents also entrenched the notion into my mind that it was always polite to introduce myself and ask others questions about the other person for good conversation. I was shy at first and didn't want to talk to others. I feared that I might say something weird and embarrass myself. I didn't want to insult another person by exposing how I really felt. In the social aspect you can't hide behind a screen of smile faces and exclamation points.

My social training continues even as recent as a few months ago at age 16. I was once at a social event with my family, and I really didn't feel like socializing. I got out my iPhone and began reading the news. My parents were not happy and told me to put the phone away. I really wanted to play with my iPhone but obeyed my parents and put the phone back in my pocket. After that event, I tried to avoid the temptation of playing with my iPhone. I have to admit that I was irritated my parents corrected me; however, I now see if they wouldn't have, I might have slid into the non-verbal communication world of only texting and email. It is easier for me to text or email versus having a face-to-face conversation because this it is an art that requires me be happy when someone is happy or to comfort someone who is sad. Really connecting with people requires me to *be all things to all people* as Paul said in 1 Corinthians 9:19.

CNN presented a study on dying conversations in young people today. "Developmental psychologists studying the impact of texting worry especially about young people, not just because kids are such promiscuous users of the technology, but because their interpersonal skills — such as they are — have not yet fully formed. Most adults were fixed social quantities when they first got their hands on a text-capable mobile device, and while their ability to have a face-to-face conversation may have eroded in recent years, it's pretty well locked in." Not so with teens. As *TIME* has reported previously: "MIT psychologist Sherry Turkle is one of the leading researchers looking into the effects of texting on interpersonal development. Turkle believes that having a conversation with another person teaches kids to, in effect, have a conversation with themselves — to think and reason and self-reflect."

According to a national study (by *CTIA* and Harris *Interactive*), "57% of teens believed that their phones were the keys to their social lives and that phones were second only to clothing when it came to a popularity status indicator."

I have a tendency to bottle up my emotions and would rather not talk. It's uncomfortable for me to admit that I'm sad or not feeling confident as I always wish to be portrayed as a confident person. Instead of talking, I would rather remain silent. This is not good because, if things are just bottled up, then there is the potential for the emotions to come out in negative ways. Medical psychology research has shown that people who cannot or will not allow themselves to experience and express their emotional pain tend to be at increased risk for serious illnesses, such as heart disease and cancer. Recently, I was upset about a minor situation and tried to hide it. Everyday I didn't talk about it and I began to feel worse. My dad recognized that I was hiding my emotions and he decided to have some one-on-one time by taking me on a favorite outing – the shooting range. As I was driving the car to the shooting range, I made some basic driving mistakes due to my emotions. Usually, I didn't make basic driving mistakes and my dad pointed that out to me. My dad then encouraged me to open up because these emotions were coming out in a negative way. Initially, I didn't believe that my dad would understand me even if I tried talking about it. It was very difficult to open up but I felt much better afterwards.

This was the perfect opportunity to practice my communication skills. For me especially I have a hard time opening up which could impact my future. I always strive to "keep my eye on the future" when tempted to shut myself in my room so to speak. I want to be a doctor and as a doctor, I need to be able to tell patients the full truth about their condition. If I don't, they may be confused and not know what to expect. I might also be attending social events and need those communication skills. Even when I'm young, I can use communication skills to my advantage. The way I communicate, especially to adults is important because I want to convey the right message of maturity. *"Take advantage of every opportunity to practice your communication skills so that when important occasions arise, you will have the gift, the style, the sharpness, the clarity, and the emotions to affect other people."* (Jim Rohn an American entrepreneur, inspirational speaker and author, 1930-2009)

When I'm trying to convey the right message, the thing I wouldn't want to do is look like a zombie and mumble my words. I must always be confident and look the other person straight in the eyes even when I don't feel confident. I don't want to fidget or squirm because this will imply that I'm nervous or don't want to be there. Even if this is the case, I can't let this show, especially if the person is a guest or a customer.

Personally, I think that everybody is a customer and we are advertising ourselves either positively or negatively. I want to be a humble, joyful servant like Jesus, who washed the feet of His disciples. I don't want to project myself as a sleepy, untidy person. I would rather be thought of as a cheerful person full of energy. *"We see our customers as invited guests to a party, and we are the hosts. It's our job every day to make every important aspect of the customer experience a little bit better."* (Jeff Bezos, CEO of *Amazon.com*, 1964-present)

I have a job as a trash boy in the River Ranch area of Lafayette Louisiana. It is a gorgeous area with New Orleans style homes and a shopping center. At my job, I am always in contact with people, and I know that the way I communicate is important because other people are creating an opinion of the company and my boss. Recently, an elderly man asked my mother if I was her son. This elderly man told my mother that I have such a great attitude and I am a hard worker. He also told my mother how he wished all teens were hard workers like me. This made my parents and me proud. I don't realize who I am influencing even when doing a part time job of picking up garbage. *"It is not the employer who pays the wages. Employers only handle the money. It is the customer who pays the wages."* (Henry Ford, American industrialist, 1883-1947)

I am a very social person but that doesn't mean I can slack off because my skills might diminish if I don't practice. Conversational abilities, just like everything else must be practiced to remain in good shape. To improve my conversation skills, my parents got me many good books to continue growing in this important area that will shape my future. One book I found helpful is *Everyone Communicates, but Few Connect* by John Maxwell. This book gave me guidelines and instruction on how to have a meaningful conversation.

Great speakers like Winston Churchill conversed every day to keep their skills sharp and in shape. If I don't practice conversational skills and only rely on texting, I will not improve in my conversation skills. I'm delighted that my communication skills can make my future brighter! *"If all my possessions were taken from me with one exception, I would choose to keep the power of communication, for by it I would soon regain all the rest"* (Daniel Webster)

Having overcome my sensory issues,
I can enjoy the beach

Chapter 7 - Staying In Line
by Managing Time

Over the years, I worked on strengthening my right hand and right leg. It was hard and sometimes seemed futile, as I didn't see much success initially. My right hand could barely lift a piece of paper and I couldn't keep my right foot straight and walk up stairs well, but I didn't give up. When I wanted to give up, my parents always encouraged me with the Bible verse: *"I can do all things through Christ who strengthens me."* (Philippians 4:13)

Many times, I was tempted to quit working on building my muscles and strength and relax. I wanted to watch TV, and play video games, instead. It was very difficult to exercise, as I would get winded easily. In order to continue growing physically and even with my education, I knew I needed to manage my time efficiently with calendars and day planners, so I could improve and strengthen my body and mind. According to an article on *discover-time-management.com*, there are five benefits to time management:

- Control
- Productivity
- Confidence
- Ability to have more fun
- Achieve goals

To manage my time, I got a calendar and planned for my daily, weekly, and monthly goals. My schedule has been effective and prevented me from becoming obsessed with distractions from my goals. Goal planning has also allowed me to be more productive, since I know what is expected of me at a given time. I know that, by having a schedule and being productive as a result, I am "keeping my eye on the future". In addition, I have a mental planner that I abide by every day. I know what I have to do, and I accomplish tasks that may not ever get done as a result. It is also comforting to know that there are iPhone apps and computer programs that can aid me in attaining my goals. Studies show advantages to taking the time to plan and write out goals. According to Harvard's *MBA Statistics Page*, in 1979, students were interviewed about goal setting. "Only 3% of the graduates had written goals and plans; 13% had goals, but they were not in writing; and a whopping 84% had no specific goals at all. Ten years later, the members of the class were interviewed again, and the findings, while somewhat predictable, were nonetheless astonishing. The 13% of the class who had goals were earning, on average, twice as much as the 84% who had no goals at all. And what about the 3% who had clear, written goals? They were earning, on average, ten times as much as the other 97% put together."

Without a schedule, I have found myself shifting my focus and even forming obsessions that took me away from my future goals. About two years ago, I lost my focus and wasted an entire summer. Since I was ahead in my studies, I took the summer off and started weight lifting. My exercise program turned into an addiction. Although, I needed weightlifting to develop my symmetry, I should have balanced my time, instead of spending hours at the gym lifting and hours reading about weight lifting. My obsession flowed into my eating habits and I thought by eating more I would gain even more muscle. My diet turned from a balanced diet with fruits, vegetables, and protein to an unbalanced diet with mostly jars of peanut butter, which resulted in an allergy that prevented me from focusing on my studies. My nose would get all stuffy and my face looked like a balloon. In the fall, when I resumed my studies, I was surprised to see my A average, turning into C's and D's. All my thoughts revolved around weight lifting, and even came before God. Weight lifting overcame my thoughts when I should have *"held all thoughts captive to the Lord"*. (2 Corinthians 10:5) My parents saw the obsessive connection and gently redirected me to a balanced schedule and diet. I regret that summer because I could have been more balanced by growing spiritually and continuing my studies, instead of only focusing on weight lifting. I ponder the words of Benjamin Franklin. *"Lost time is never found again"*

I definitely saw the importance of planning and schedules two summers ago when I was addicted to fitness. My summer was wasted and I couldn't honestly say that I had made any accomplishments. *"Determine never to be idle. No person will have occasion to complain of the want of time, who never loses any. It is wonderful how much may be done, if we are always doing."* (Thomas Jefferson)

I am also more aware that seemingly good habits can slowly begin to consume me. My addiction started slowly and drew me in little by little. I wasn't aware the addiction overtook me because it happened slowly. I started with a balanced form of exercise and lifted three times a week and then it moved up to a daily routine for hours of lifting and hours consumed with reading articles about weight lifting. I didn't think about anything else. Today, I ask myself what I spend my time thinking about. I want my thoughts to be guided by God. Our time on this earth is so short, and I want to make ever minute glorify God. As Confucius once said, *"Time flows away like the water in the river."*

By "keeping my eye on the future," I have come to realize the importance of having a schedule and by keeping my mind focused on the direction God has planned for me. *"Thy word is a lamp unto thy feet, and a light unto my path.* (Psalm 119:105*)* If I organize and listen to God's guidance, my life will remain balanced. I also like the words of Benjamin Franklin, *"Dost thou love life? Then do not squander time, for that is the stuff life is made of"*.

If we love our life, we will love our time also because, according to Doc Childre and Howard Martin, authors of *"The HeartMath Solution"*: *"You're writing the story of your life one moment at a time."*

Horseback riding helped me to develop strong legs enabling me to run a mini-triathlon

Chapter 8 - Feeling Cool With Music

When I was about 2 years old, I still wasn't walking, nor was I talking due to Cerebral Palsy that weakened my right side and initially impacted my speech. To keep my right hand, open, the occupational therapist, made a brace for my fingers. I wore that brace for many years, as well as a brace on my right foot to keep it straight. While my left foot was straight, my right foot was weak and pointed out to the side. My parents would buy me 2 sizes of shoes – one larger for my left foot and a smaller one for my right since my foot was smaller. The physical therapists and occupational therapists had a difficult job with me. Not only did I scream all the time due to sensory issues, I also could not be motivated to walk, exercise my hand, or even talk. After praying for wisdom: *"If any of you lacks wisdom, he should ask God who gives generously* (James 1:5), my parents found a motivating factor– music.

My parents found that classical music calmed me, and Christian children's songs made me happy. When my occupational and physical therapists were at a loss as to motivate me, my mother told them to sing to George.

When my parents recognized the driving force of music, they signed me up for ballet with my sister. As a young man, I am a bit embarrassed to admit that I was in ballet, while most of my friends were in football, soccer, and basketball. At times, I was even made fun of for doing ballet, which hurt my feelings. However, it was comforting to know that even football players use ballet to strengthen and improve their game and there are many successful and masculine male ballet dancers. According to an article on *ehow.com*: "Ballet works many muscle groups, including your core, arms, chest, shoulders, back, hamstrings, quadriceps and calves."

The musical environment of ballet motivated me and helped me to strengthen my muscles. I had a fabulous teacher, Ms. Beverly Spell, owner of The Ballet Studio in Milton and Lafayette, Louisiana, who worked on strengthening my arm and leg. Ms. Spell did not go easy on me and required the same stretches and movements as the other dancers. Today, I am glad my parents saw the benefits of ballet for my strength. Athletes, today, are noticing great benefits when practicing ballet. According to an article on *Healthy Living*: "Professional football players such as Vance Johnson and Akili Smith even attribute ballet to their overall success on the field. Flexibility is very important in football despite the fact that the sport is often seen as a strength-centric activity. Flexibility helps players to avoid tackles and make catches and can reduce the likelihood of injuries to joints such as the knees and shoulders. Ballet relies on flexibility to create graceful movements, so football players who study ballet receive training that increases their flexibility beyond what they would likely receive performing standard football training drills and exercises. NFL Hall of Fame member Lynn Swann even credits his graceful performance in games in part to flexibility that he learned from ballet training and other dance classes, adding that this training helped him achieve body control, balance and a sense of rhythm and timing."

Music kept me moving when I otherwise would not have exercised.

According to an article on *eMed Expert*: "Music is one of the few activities that involves the whole brain. It is intrinsic to all cultures and can have surprising benefits not only for learning language, improving memory and focusing attention, but also for physical coordination and development.

Listening to music or playing an instrument can actually make you learn better. And research confirms this.

Scientific studies show that music has the power to enhance certain kinds of higher brain function: reading and literacy skills; spatial-temporal reasoning; and mathematical abilities. Even children with attention deficit/hyperactivity disorder benefit in mathematics tests from listening to music beforehand.

Music reduces muscle tension and improves body movement and coordination. Music may play an important role in developing, maintaining and restoring physical functioning in the rehabilitation of persons with movement disorders."

My parents found these studies to be true when encouraging me with music. My mood improved. I began walking when I was two-and-a half years old and my focus improved as before I had a hard time focusing on reading or any lengthy activity like block building.

My parents continue playing classical music while we study, read, and learn throughout the day. I found it relaxing and helped me to focus.

When I was a teenager, I thought that I had to listen to a certain type of music to be cool. I listened to some rock and rap and found the music distracting and impacted my mood. I personally don't like the lyrics and beat of rock and rap; it isn't in line with my personality.

I have since discovered that I do not have to "fit in" to be cool. *"Respect yourself and others will respect you."* (Confucius) I believe that I can be cool in my own sense listening to the type of music that I like. Everyone has his or her particular reasons for liking a given type of music. For me, I like certain pop music because it is upbeat. There are some songs that have bad language. However, on the AOL radio app there is a feature that will block curse words, which I use extensively to combat that fact. *"Music produces a kind of pleasure which human nature cannot do without."* (Confucius)

According to a new study by the nonprofit Pacific Institute for Research and Evaluation: "If you listen to rap music, you're more likely to use alcohol and drugs and to behave in an aggressive." In this study, more than 1,200 California community-college students ages 15-25 took part— titled *Music, Substance Use and Aggression* - and answered survey questions about their music-listening habits, use of alcohol and drugs and 'aggressive behaviors,' such as fighting or threatening people with violence The results found that almost 70% of the students who listened to music 'daily or almost daily,' listened to rap and hip-hop, and when that data was compared with the students' answers about alcohol, drugs and violence, the survey found that 'substance use and aggressive behaviors among young people were significantly associated to certain genres of popular music, mainly rap, reggae, rock and techno.'"

An article on *Science Daily* found that the reference to drugs in rap songs had increased six fold since 1979 and that these references are no longer the cautionary tales they used to be. Today, they are vivid stories praising the use of illegal drugs. For me, lyrics linger in my head, and I want my brain to be focused on positive lyrics that will help my future. This verse made me stop and think about the music I want lingering in my mind: *"Finally, brothers, whatever is true, whatever is honorable, whatever is just, whatever is pure, whatever is lovely, whatever is commendable, if there is any excellence, if there is anything worthy of praise, think about these things."* (Philippians 4:8)

I realized how influential music could be when I started to like the theme song of the movie *Narnia*. I liked it because it created a sense of courage within me making me want to face my challenges. As a result of realizing how influential music can be, I also realized that I could manipulate music for my benefit and saw the dangers of listening to negative music. I would experience negative feelings when I listened to heavy metal rock and saw the connection. I knew that if I didn't manipulate my music selections, my future could be entirely different from the one I want it to be. *If I were not a physicist, I would probably be a musician. I often think in music. I live my daydreams in music. I see my life in terms of music."* (Albert Einstein)

I also realized that I would never be able to succeed in life if I listened to negative music. I know that when I listen to a negative song, I create a negative opinion of something on my mind. I realized that I was "keeping my eye on the future" by regulating the type of music that entered my head. In doing this, I am removing a roadblock to my future success.

I believe that, as long as I realize the powerful effects of music and structure my listening habits accordingly, then I can use my chosen music to aid me in the road to success. Music is a tool that can be tapped and used to my advantage. *"Music isn't just a pleasure, a transient satisfaction. It's a need, a deep hunger; and when the music is right, it's joy. Love. A foretaste of heaven. A comfort in grief.* (Orson Scott, American author and speaker)

I continue to work on making the right decisions with my music but I now know that, by controlling what I hear, I indicate that I don't want a life that isn't in line with my dreams. By regulating what I believe, I make my future dreams possible. *"Let the word of Christ dwell in you richly, teaching and admonishing one another in all wisdom, singing psalms and hymns and spiritual songs, with thankfulness in your hearts to God."* (Colossians 3:16)

I worked hard on developing fine motor skills to strengthen my weak right hand.

George's strong muscles made Grandma Day feel safe when helping her to walk.

Chapter 9 - Defeating the Dragons
of Addiction

When I was young, my parents tried to instill balance in all areas of my life. My parent's talk about their own addictions and obsessiveness that they worked on throughout the years. Before my parents married, both used to work at a software company putting in over 12 hours a day, 7 days-a-week, even on the holidays. My parents saw this was not a good balance and slowly overcame this addiction by adding more relaxation and by volunteering for church events. As a result of my parents working on balance in their lives, they were able to help me. When I was a toddler, I struggled with food addiction to macaroni and applesauce, not wanting to eat anything else. Even though, I screamed and cried, they worked to encouraging me to eat vegetables and protein. My parents persistence paid off and my health improved with good nutrition.

Throughout the years, my addictions continue. In every case, I would pray for the *"Holy Spirit's fruit of self-control"* needed in every area of my life.

Occasionally, I struggled with an addiction to chocolate. I have a hard time resisting that sweet taste which made me come back to the pantry for more. I personally never intend for anything to become an addiction. It just happens little by little. I always need to stay awake to the dangers of an addiction. *"So then, let us not be like others, who are asleep, but let us be alert and self-controlled."* (1 Thessalonians 5:6)

I am aware of my potential for possible, future addictions such as smoking. I try to avoid situations that could lead me to smoke, which I know would lure me in and cause an addiction that I would later regret. According to an article on *Myaddiction.com*, the effects of nicotine are so powerful that: "Half the number of teens who start smoking will continue for another fifteen to twenty years."

Statistics by the *Center for Disease Control*, shows that: "Approximately 440,000 Americans die each year from diseases related to smoking; About 90% of all smokers started as teen smokers; 90% of the above 440,000 are teen smokers; Every day, 6,000 children under the age of 18 start smoking. Of those, 2,000 will keep smoking. That's 800,000 new teen smokers every year! If current tobacco use patterns continue, an estimated 6.4 million children will die prematurely from a smoking-related disease. Unfortunately, the reason that there are more teen smokers is that they become addicted faster and on lower levels of nicotine than adults."

As I grow and mature, I see that I have to be aware in all areas of my life to practice self-control. The following verse shows me how I can fall if tempted into an addiction: *Like a city whose walls are broken through is a person who lacks self-control.* (Proverbs 25:28)

I have shared my struggles with food and an obsession with weight lifting, but this addiction may have gone unnoticed and may have even gotten worse if I wouldn't have tackled it. This addiction, although difficult for me to talk about, is necessary so I can possibly help others avoid it. The addiction I am leading up to is pornography. When I was about 12 years old, I enjoyed reading books about history. One book was a European Renaissance book with pictures of naked sculptures. To most people, this seems harmless, but the images overtook me and I desired to look at the images frequently. During that time of history, people viewed the body as a work of art. Hence, they created many nude men and women sculptures and paintings. I believe that the body is a wonderful creation, but I need to guard my eyes from viewing any nudity. I recognized my obsession because my parents always taught us to be modest and maintain pure thoughts and image. Although these Renaissance books are easily available at bookstores, I decided to overcome this addiction by going to another section of the bookstore. I was successful defeating my addiction to porn.

My parents monitored my Internet closely so I was not able to view pornography on the Internet. According to a study on *Covenant Eyes*: "93% of boys and 62% of girls view internet pornography before the age of 18." Other statistics show that: "79% of youth are exposed to pornography in the home and the largest group of viewers of Internet porn is children between ages 12 and 17."

Some think pornography can be easily viewed in the privacy of their home, without anyone even noticing. *"For whatever is in secret will be brought into the open and everything concealed will be brought to light and made known to all."* (Luke 8:17) All sin, pornography included, has many side effects, including the tearing down of a person's spirituality. According to an article on *A Battle Plan*, "Pornography amplifies selfishness; Pornography focuses on our satisfaction, our needs, and turns us towards ourselves; Women become objects instead of human beings; Pornography takes control of our passion and uses it to satisfy itself. Your passions will get consumed by it and you have no desire left to pursue noble causes; pornography will destroy your ability to be intimate (emotionally & physically) with your spouse and emotionally with others."

Unfortunately, pornography is big business and it's hard not to see advertisements because they're everywhere. According to *Internet Filter Review*: "Every second, $3,075.64 is being spent on pornography, 28,258 Internet viewers are viewing pornography, 372 Internet users are typing adult search terms into search engines, and every 39 minutes, a new pornographic video is made in the United States." If I am not careful, pornography is going to lure me in. I want to avoid any immorality, which would cause my spiritual downfall and keep me from the success of my future. *"Flee from sexual immorality. Every other sin a person commits is outside the body, but the sexually immoral person sins against his own body."* (1 Corinthians 6:18)

I am thankful that I had a close relationship with my parents and was able to share my pornography addiction with my dad. It was embarrassing, but my dad comforted me. In addition, my dad encouraged me telling me he could be my accountability partner. As an accountability partner, my dad and I check with each other that we are remaining holy by looking at, reading, and watching only holy entertainment. Some of my friends have their youth pastors, uncles, family friends, priests, or spiritual directors as an accountability partner and have seen great results. *"Though one may be overpowered, two can defend themselves. A cord of three strands is not quickly broken."* (Ecclesiastes 4:12)

According to a *Yahoo* article: "Numerous research studies across all walks of life have shown that having a partner, someone to hold you accountable, will help you to succeed with whatever task you are trying to accomplish. Whether you're dieting or quitting smoking, having someone specific to be your accountability partner will increase your chances of success considerably. If you are a Christian, an accountability partner can make a huge difference in your relationship with Jesus Christ. Accountability partners can be extremely helpful in any Christian's life." *"As iron sharpens iron, so one person sharpens another."* (Proverbs 27:17)

My dad also took away any temptation on the computer by installing a website blocker. This not only blocked pornography but also drugs, violence, and gambling. To avoid any temptations on the computer, my parents also have a rule that computers and TV's are not to be used in our bedroom. The computer can only be used in the dining room where there are a lot of people. With a lot of people around, I am not tempted to search the Internet for inappropriate material. One statistic from *Enough is Enough* showed that having a computer in the bedroom adds temptation for kids and teens. "Nearly one-third (31%) of 8 to 18-year-olds have a computer in their bedroom, and one in five (20%) have an Internet connection. Forty-two percent of Internet users aged 10 to 17 surveyed said they had seen online pornography in a recent 12-month span. Of those, 66% said they did not want to view the images and had not sought them out."

The filters are annoying at times because they block sites that are all right but I still think that they're worth having because of their primary function. *"Put to death therefore what is earthly in you: sexual immorality, impurity, passion, evil desire, and covetousness, which is idolatry."* (Colossians 3:5)

My parents and I created a plan that successful got me out of the bondage of addiction. I am relieved and glad that I can talk with my parents about any issue that affects my life. An article by the author of the study, Sonya Thompson concluded: "Parents need to improve dialogue with their children and their own awareness level. They need to be the ones setting the boundaries in the house." Since then, I have not had any problems with immodest pictures. If I had no plan, my attempts at riding myself of the addiction might have been futile. It hit me that an addiction must be treated like everything else in life.

There must be structure, order and a plan when dealing with these circumstances. If I want to be a successful doctor, there needs to be a plan detailing how I will become doctor. If I want to overcome a challenge, I can't just shoot at it, and hope I obtain the results. The following verse encourages me to stay strong in self-control. *"Therefore, prepare your minds for action; be self-controlled; set your hope fully on the grace to be given you when Jesus Christ is revealed."* (1 Peter 1:13)

Addictions are like the wind as teens zoom downhill on their emotional rollercoaster. They seem harmless at first but then balloon into giant fire breathing monsters that threaten to scorch us. *"Addiction is a decision. An individual wants something, whatever that something is, and makes a decision to get it. Once they have it, they make a decision to take it. If they take it too often, that process of decision-making gets out of control, and if it gets far out of control, it becomes an addiction. At that point the decision is a difficult one to make, but it is still a decision. Do I or don't I. Am I going to take or am I not going to waste my life or am I going to say no and try and stay sober and be a decent person. It is a decision. Each and every time. A decision. String enough of those decisions together and you set a course and you set a standard of living."* (James Frey, American writer)

George entertains residents
at a local nursing home.

Chapter 10 - Understanding the Golden Rule of School

With my right side weakness, my parents researched the Montessori program that involved hands on learning. The program seemed to be a good match for me, which would require the use of my weakened right hand and right leg. When I was 3 years old, my parents enrolled me in the Valley Forge Montessori near Philadelphia. The owners, Mr. and Mrs. Kelly did much to help me and were very patient when I had fits about things such as wanting to get into the car myself. In addition, my teacher Ms. Phelen was tough and loving as she treated me like the other students and not like a student with a disability. Ms. Phelen told my mother she was doing too much for me. Although, this hurt my mother's feelings, she took her words to heart and tried not to do as much for me. With this new "tough love" teaching, I started improving, getting stronger, and gaining confidence. A week after I started the Montessori, I got the courage to walk up the stairs. Until that time, I was still crawling up the stairs because my weaker leg and foot did not have enough coordination. The "hands-on" learning was perfect for my learning style. *"A mind without instruction can no more bear fruit than can a field, however fertile, without cultivation."* (Cicero)

About a year later, we moved to Louisiana and my parents enrolled me in a private school for pre-K and Kindergarten. Both my teachers and parents noticed I had a different learning style not conducive for a classroom. After I learned to talk when I was close to 3 years old, I didn't stop talking. I asked questions about everything and wanted more and more information. Throughout the class, I talked and asked questions and couldn't stay quiet. Inside I would want to burst because I had so many questions, and I had to stay quiet. For example, our class would study the bald eagle. The teacher gave appropriate information for a kindergartener but I wanted more and more information. The class was not designed for spending hours on one subject so the teacher had to move on to another topic. This left me unhappy and very grumpy. My love for learning was diminishing and my parents began to notice the results.

In addition, I had a hard time with transitions in the classroom. For example, if math lasted one hour and I was having so much fun and really getting into math, I didn't want to switch to Phonics. I would act out and scream. The teachers thought I was being defiant and reprimanded both my parents and me for my actions. I didn't mean to have tantrums, I just really enjoyed the subject I was working on and did not want to switch to another one at the time. I had a hard time controlling my emotions.

In Kindergarten, I started to have a substantial amount of homework and this concerned my parents, as I didn't have time to play and strengthen my right hand and right leg. With additional homework, I didn't even have time to play the piano as much. My parents were concerned that this imbalance would be great impedance to my success in life.

My learning style was not conducive to this private school and my parents prayed for direction.

God placed many homeschool families in my parent's path prior to this decision. My parents met homeschoolers in Philadelphia, Nebraska, Florida, and know many wonderful families in Louisiana. My mother's friend, Jane Jurek, had a huge impact on my mother, bringing her books and encouragement telling her that she could do it. My parents felt that the decision to homeschool was like jumping off a cliff. It was frightening but my parents leaned on the verse, *"God did not give you a spirit of fear but of power, love, and a sound mind."* (2 Timothy 1:7)

"In 1997, a study of 5,402 homeschool students from 1,657 families was released. It was entitled, *Strengths of Their Own: Home Schoolers Across America.* The study demonstrated that homeschoolers, on average, out-performed their counterparts in the public schools by 30 to 37 percentile points in all subjects. A significant finding when analyzing the data for 8th graders was the evidence that homeschoolers who are homeschooled two or more years score substantially higher than students who have been homeschooled one year or less. The new homeschoolers were scoring, on average, in the 59th percentile compared to students homeschooled the last two or more years who scored between 86th and 92nd percentile.

This was confirmed in another study by Dr. Lawrence Rudner of 20,760 homeschooled students which found the homeschoolers who have homeschooled all their school aged years had the highest academic achievement. This was especially apparent in the higher grades. This is a good encouragement to families catch the long-range vision and homeschool through high school.

Another important finding of *Strengths of Their Own* was that the race of the student did not make any difference. There was no significant difference between minority and white homeschooled students. For example, in grades K-12, both white and minority students scored, on the average, in the 87th percentile. In math, whites scored in the 82nd percentile while minorities scored in the 77th percentile. In the public schools, however, there is a sharp contrast. White public school eighth grade students, nationally scored the 58th percentile in math and the 57th percentile in reading. Black eighth grade students, on the other hand, scored on the average at the 24th percentile in math and the 28th percentile in reading. Hispanics scored at the 29th percentile in math and the 28th percentile in reading."

After I had started homeschooling, I gradually began to like learning. My parents got me books on my favorite topics. Daily, my mom snuggled between me and my sister, Emily, on the couch and required us to read for an hour a day. My parents set up reading lights on the bed, so we could read before we went to sleep and did not allow a TV or computer in our bedroom.

According to an article in the *New York Times*: "Children with bedroom TVs score lower on school tests and are more likely to have sleep problems. Having a television in the bedroom is strongly associated with being overweight and also comes with a higher risk for smoking. *The Journal of Pediatrics* reported that preschool children with bedroom TVs were more likely to be overweight. In a 2005 study in *The Archives of Pediatric and Adolescent Medicine*, researchers looked at the television, computer and video game habits of almost 400 children in six Northern California schools for a year. About 70% of the children in the study had their own TV in the bedroom; they scored significantly and consistently lower on math, reading and language-arts tests. Another October study, published in *Pediatrics*, showed that kindergartners with bedroom TVs had more sleep problems."

At times, my parents seemed strict. A lot of my friends had televisions and computers in their room and I thought it was unfair that I could only read. Now, I am thankful to parents, and I can't put down my schoolbooks. I started reading so much that I surpassed my grade level and in junior high, I was reading at a college level. *"Do not train a child to learn by force or harshness; but direct them to it by what amuses their minds, so that you may be better able to discover with accuracy the peculiar bent of the genius of each."* (Plato)

My parents tried to make learning fun and made learning everywhere not just with schoolbooks. During the day, we would take a break from our studies and my mother would take us to get fresh vegetables and fruits from a local market. My mother pointed out prices per pound so our math expanded. At this market, we became friends with the owners and managers, and they let us help ring up the customers while my mother shopped. Again, we experienced fun hands-on math lessons. I loved receiving the payments, putting them in the cash register and then counting out the change! *"Tell me and I forget, teach me and I may remember, involve me and I learn."* (Benjamin Franklin) Hands-on learning helped me retain knowledge because I wasn't just memorizing facts for the sake of a good grade. *"I have been impressed with the urgency of doing. Knowing is not enough; we must apply. Being willing is not enough; we must do."* (Leonardo da Vinci)

My daily school schedule was set up with a combination of structure and personal selection. I knew how many pages and subjects that needed to be accomplished but I was able to choose which subject to do first and if I needed assistance, my mother would help. My mom provided classical music throughout the day to create a peaceful, creative environment. My parents encouraged us with incentives. For example, if my sister and I completed all our school, piano lessons, and chores such as making beds, clearing the dishwasher, picking up toys…then we were able to watch a favorite DVD or play a special educational computer game. If we accomplished all our chores and homework joyfully throughout the week, we were treated to a trip to the zoo or ice cream or a toy from the "Dollar General" store. This structure enabled me to know what was expected of me and encouraged me to work hard because I really liked the treats. Later, my parents included allowance for chores and extra schoolwork. This was especially motivating to me because I could save for toys I wanted to buy.

I am very fortunate that my life has been stable. My parents have always been supportive. Especially as a young person, I need this stability in order to learn and progress. According to an article in the *New York Times:* "Students with strong academic abilities and supportive parents are basically guaranteed to graduate. Remedial students who benefit from involved, proactive parents are likely to earn a diploma. Conversely, dedicated students who possess good academic skills can possibly graduate despite living with uninvolved parents or in dysfunctional home environments. However, students with poor academic skills who also suffer from a lack of parental involvement or support have virtually no chance of graduating from high school."

My love for learning grew in my nurturing environment. I was able to feel the feeling of achievement a college student feels because I could honestly say that I had mastered a subject. I had not just been rushed through the course barely understanding the topic and stressing that I might have gotten a C. Today, my dream is to be a neurologist, which might have been an impossible one if I hadn't developed a love for learning.

As a teenager, I am trying to be careful about distractions that could keep me from my goal such as girlfriends. I have lots of friends that are girls, but I feel called to wait until I reach my career to have a girlfriend so I can have the funds to support a family.

Recent research on the *Effects of Romantic Relationships on Academic Performance* showed that teen dating negatively effects education. Academic performances are affected by teen dating because of pressure, drama, and loss of focus. Teen dating could also decrease grades and test scores."

I need to also balance my extra-curricular activities such as weight lifting and piano so that my main emphasis is on my studies. In my opinion, there are three main components to my life: studies, extra-curricular activities, and social life. By "keeping my eye on the future," I realize that I will reach my goal of being a doctor only if I balance my priorities. Studies for me are the most important thing and thus I must be disciplined restricting the other two for the benefit of my studies. *"Seek freedom and become captive of your desires. Seek discipline and find your liberty."* (Frank Herbert, successful American science fiction writer, 1920-86)

By disciplined myself, I am prepared not only for the challenges of my life now but in the future as well. I would get stuck in a rut trying to devote equal amounts of my time to two of the three aspects and making no headway if it weren't for my parents. They definitely did their jobs establishing structure and discipline in the house early creating a very effective learning environment. *"The ability to discipline yourself to delay gratification in the short term in order to enjoy greater rewards in the long term, is the indispensable prerequisite for success."* (Brian Tracy)

Today, I thrive on discipline and structure getting up at 5 am to start school. Since I have specific goals for my future, I want to get a lot of studies accomplished so I can be successful for college. Some days it isn't easy, I just felt sick of going through the same, sometimes boring routine. I wanted to get out of the house and be done with school. However, I saw the necessity of "keeping my eye on the future" every day.

In order to get up at 5 a.m., I also have an early bed habit so my body is used to rest at a specific time. As Benjamin Franklin said, *"Early to bed, early to rise, makes a man healthy, wealthy, and wise."* My parents saw the importance of regular sleep patterns for my health and focus in school at an early age and required me to be in bed by 8 p.m. In fact, an early sleeping schedule is linked to a reduced threat of depression in teens. In an article on *livestrong.com,* the reasons are made obvious. "A team of U.S. psychiatric professionals led by James E. Gangwisch, Ph.D., conducted a large-scale study to assess the impact of parentally dictated bedtimes on the incidence of depression and suicidal ideation among teenagers. The team's survey covered more than 15,500 adolescents in grades 7 to 12. In an early 2010 issue of *Sleep*, researchers reported that teens with parental set bedtimes of midnight or later were 24% more likely to suffer from depression and 20% more likely to consider suicide than teens with parental set bedtimes of 10 p.m. or earlier. Researchers concluded that earlier bedtimes generally lengthen overall sleep duration and thus are protective against mood disorders in adolescents."

I want to make my waking hours as productive as I can and thus strive to maintain an early and regular bedtime. At times, it was a bit irritating having to go to bed early because I couldn't participate in as many extra-curricular activities. However, my parents were always reminding me of the benefits of plenty of sleep.

According to an *ABC* article, "Studies have found that children who had established bedtimes had higher math and literacy skills. Inconsistent bedtimes can lead to homemade jet lag or the de-synchronization of the two systems that regulate sleep -- the circadian rhythm and the homeostatic pressure system. Just staying up three hours later on weekends is the equivalent to flying across three time zones every weekend. School-age children between age 5 and 12 need 9 to 11 hours. Adolescents need eight and a half to nine and a half hours." According to University of Minnesota's Dr. Kyla Wahlstrom: "A motivated student can sacrifice sleep to maintain high GPAs, but he or she may pay for that success with higher levels of depression and stress. In addition, teen boys who have a high number of extracurricular activities are significantly more likely to be involved in a fall-asleep car crash."

My parents also recognized that having an early bed routine for the children meant having time together to talk and grow in their marriage. Any relationship requires structure and work to maintain a close marriage. My parents regularly have "date nights" and this routine has made them a happy couple and happy parents make for happy kids!

According to a study found in the article *Save Your Marriage –Get Your Child to Sleep*: "when kids go to sleep at a reasonable hour - 7-8

PM - marriages are happier and more fulfilled than those whose kids are up until 11 PM.

When kids go to sleep too late, parents simply don't have any time to refuel themselves or their relationships. It seems as though they're parenting 24 hours a day, and once the kids are asleep, the parents just conk out themselves. Too often, parents think they're doing their children a service by allowing them to do what they want in the bedtime arena. However, ultimately, if mom and dad fall apart, the children suffer. A happy parental marriage is one of the highest indicators of ultimate happiness in children. Without sleep, parents feel cranky with their children, with one another, and become resentful of the parental duties they're expected to perform day after day."

My parent's example and discipline in a structured environment has helped me at an early age. I have adopted those disciplines and apply thenm to my everyday life to achieve a successful future. If God calls me to marry, I also plan to make time for my wife and have an early bedtime routine for my children.

Even though I had less time for other activities, I came to enjoy going to bed early because I had a nightlight and was able to read. Today, I have a love for reading, which I probably wouldn't have developed if I hadn't had the opportunity to read prior to going to sleep. *"Learn from yesterday, live for today, hope for tomorrow. The important thing is to not stop questioning."* (Albert Einstein)

Dr. Laura Markham, a clinical psychologist, states that: "Routines give children a sense of security and helps them develop self-discipline. Structure and routines teach kids how to constructively control themselves and their environments. Kids who come from chaotic homes where belongings aren't put away never learn that life can run more smoothly if things are organized a little. In homes where there is no set time or space to do homework, kids never learn how to sit themselves down to accomplish an unpleasant task. Kids who don't develop basic self-care routines, from grooming to food, may find it hard to take care of themselves as young adults. Structure allows us to internalize constructive habits. A predictable routine allows children to feel safe, and to develop a sense of mastery in handling their lives. As this sense of mastery is strengthened, they can tackle larger changes: walking to school by themselves, and paying for a purchase at the store. Routines help kids learn to take charge of their own activities. Over time, kids learn to brush their teeth, pack their backpacks, etc., without constant reminders. Kids love being in charge of themselves. This feeling increases their sense of mastery and competence. Kids who feel more independent and in charge of themselves have less need to rebel and be oppositional."

My early structure and the reward system pushed me when I didn't have the desire to study. I used to bump along in school. I would get the required amount complete and do no more because I had no real passion for it. All of the books just seemed dry containing useless information at one point. I was just going through the motions not really seeing the value of my education. Then one day I realized, as I studied my biology, "you know this biology can help me in the future because I want to be a doctor," I had found a reason to learn. *"Education is the kindling of a flame, not the filling of a vessel."* (Socrates) I had found it within myself to enjoy school and see its benefits.

My smaller right hand and leg made shopping for clothes difficult.

Education should always have a key place in our lives. Even when we're young we should entertain the thought of getting a college education. Warren Buffett was earning a solid salary as a newspaper deliveryman and initially didn't plan on going to college. Fortunately for him, his father pushed the issue and so he decided to go. Despite working full time, he graduated in only three years. Today, he's one of the wealthiest people in the world. His college education had paid off! *"The minute you stop making mistakes is the minute you stop learning."* (Miley Cyrus)

"I can do ALL things through Christ who strengthens me." -Philippians 4:13

Chapter 11 - Man-Made Bridges
To The Future

There were many times when I got discouraged with things such as learning to dive off a diving board. As I stood there looking down at the water for the seemingly millionth time, I wondered if I would ever get it. I was fearful and I didn't know if my body would have the strength to swim to the ledge after actually diving in. My parents were always cheering me on when I felt like caving in and when it seemed hopeless to continue trying to dive, swim, walk, and even read. People have always been there for me always encouraging me when I was down. At times, I have felt very sad and all alone in my endeavors. Seeing this, my parents surrounded me with mentors, educators, encouragers, and friends that told me *"I could do ALL things through Christ who strengthens me."* (Philippians 4:13)

I'm comforted knowing there are others who have gone through similar physical challenges. I am inspired by Bethany Hamilton from the movie *Soul Surfer*. After losing her arm at age 13 in a shark attack, she tackled an intense challenge- having to learn to surf with one arm in order to surf competitively again. Two years later, she won first place in the Explorer Women's Division of the *NSSA National Championship*s. Bethany's lack of symmetry did not stop her from reaching her goals of a successful surfer and a role model to many.

Another inspiration is Charles Woodson, an American football cornerback for the Green Bay Packers who was born with a clubfoot. Charles had to wear braces until he was 4 years old to fix the problem. He played college football at the University of Michigan for the Michigan Wolverines. In 1997, Charles led the Wolverines to a share of the national championship. He is the only primarily defensive player to have won the Heisman Trophy. On April 26, 2006, Charles and the Green Bay Packers reached a 7-year contract agreement that could be worth as much as $52.7 million with bonuses and incentives.

Another example is Joni Eareckson Tada, who enjoyed riding horses, hiking, tennis, and swimming as a teenager. On July 30, 1967, she dove into Chesapeake Bay after misjudging the shallowness of the water. She suffered a fracture between the fourth and fifth cervical levels and became a quadriplegic, paralyzed from the shoulders down. During her two years of rehabilitation, according to her autobiography, Joni experienced anger, depression, suicidal thoughts, and religious doubts. However, Joni learned to paint with a brush between her teeth, and began selling her artwork. To date, she has written over 40 books, recorded several musical albums, starred in an autobiographical movie of her life, and is an advocate for disabled people. Joni founded *Joni and Friends* (JAF) in 1979, an organization for Christian ministry in the disabled community throughout the world. In 2006, the *Joni and Friends International Disability Centre* in Agoura California was established.

There are countless examples of people who have inspired me to keep working to build up my strength. These people helped to instill a confidence that enabled me to conquer and continue to conquer my challenges.

A close family friend, Katie Jones, from Philadelphia, inspired me when I was young. My parents met Katie at the church's nursery where she was helping to babysit during mass. Katie's enthusiasm and work ethic inspired my parents. Jones, who did not have a left arm, wore a prosthesis. Jones accomplished as much if not more than the other girls around her. My parents hired Katie to help, as a mother's assistant to care for my sister and me. Jones played soccer, danced ballet, baked the best brownies, and is a talented artist. After we moved, Katie worked jobs to pay for a ticket to fly down to visit us at the age of 13. I never thought of Katie having only one arm because she did everything without help from curling her hair, putting on a necklace, baking great Italian dishes...everything! When Katie went to college, she drove in heavy traffic through Philadelphia on a regular basis. One semester, she even studied abroad in Europe. Katie graduated from college and worked for Hallmark and then QVC. Recently, she married and was a beautiful bride. Katie Jones is one my hero's and inspired me to live life to the fullest.

I continuously seek out role models to inspire me and encourage me to grow. The examples of good role models give me hope to keep going when I want to stop. In addition, positive mentors in my life provide me with wisdom needed to reach my goals. *"Role models who push us to exceed our limits, physical training that removes our spare tires, and risks that expand our sphere of comfortable action are all examples of eustress—stress that is healthful and the stimulus for growth."* (Timothy Ferriss, American author and entrepreneur)

According to the *National Mentor Partnership*, "Mentoring is a positive youth development strategy that supports the goal of reducing the dropout rate by 50% over the next five years. Research has shown that mentoring has significant positive effects on two early indicators of high school dropouts: high levels of absenteeism (Kennelly & Monrad, 2007) and recurring behavior problems (Thurlow, Sinclair & Johnson, 2002). A landmark *Public/Private Ventures* evaluation of *Big Brothers Big Sisters* programs showed that students who meet regularly with their mentors are 52% less likely than their peers to skip a day of school. An analysis of mentoring program evaluations conducted by Jekielek, Moore and Hair found that youth in mentoring relationships present better attitudes and behaviors at school and are more likely to attend college than their counterparts."

My greatest mentors are my parents, in addition to family members, friends, priests, youth pastors, teachers, and personal trainers.

When I started weightlifting, I looked up to all my big muscular friends and absorbed their advice. One trainer I learned a lot from is Jacob Azenne from City Club. Jacob set me up on a weight-training program to grow my muscles and corrected my form so I would avoid injuries. Jacob's knowledge and encouragement helped me to get stronger and gain symmetry and muscle on both my left and right side. I look back at when I started and see the progress of muscle strength and mass due to Jacob's guidance. I have gained more muscle, and my body has become more defined. My bench press has gone from 45 pounds to 215 pounds. The weight on the squatting exercise has gone from 45 to 230 pound. My leg press increased from about 90 pounds to over 300. I continually try to increase my weight and reps for the various exercises and try to make myself better.

I also had good mentors who encouraged me in the field of medicine: my uncles Mike Ford and Michael Day. My uncle, Mike Ford, a dermatologist, patiently explained in-depth medical procedures in his field while giving me tours of his office showing me slides of cancer cells under his microscopes. Uncle Mike's enthusiasm for his job and his excitement to share his knowledge with me inspired me to explore the field of medicine.

My uncle, Michael Day, worked in the ER and then later opened a private general practice. Although he works long hours, my uncle continues working even on vacations. An avid scuba diver, my Uncle Michael travels to Truk Island, north of New Guinea, to shoot underwater photography. Uncle Michael brings his medical expertise to the people of Truk Island, while vacationing, where he provides medicine to prevent malaria.

Mentors were all around me so they were never very hard to find. If I couldn't find a mentor in a particular area, I would search one out at the library or bookstore by reading autobiographies and books by well-known people in the field. However, I believe that it's always better to get the advice of someone in person rather than read autobiographies. For example, I went through a stock market craze a couple of years ago and contemplated what to buy. A neighbor, who had much experience with the stock market, offered advice, which I gladly accepted. The reason I did was because he was much more knowledgeable about the market than I am. My neighbor and inventor, has over 20 patents and has been investing in the stock market for years. I was relieved that I had the knowledge necessary to make a good purchase.

Through all the challenges I have faced, I have relied heavily on others from physical therapists, coaches, parents and friends.

I have found that older people have a great wealth of wisdom even though as a teenager I sometimes think I know everything there is to know. Adults are in a position of authority and personally, I always find it better when I at least consider their advice before tackling a challenge. *"Let every person be subject to the governing authorities. For there is no authority except from God, and those that exist have been instituted by God."* (Romans 13:1)

I continue to seek the advice and wisdom of those around me to help accomplish my goals. I can honestly say that I couldn't have done what I did without the help of my friends, teachers, coaches, trainers, neighbors, physical therapists, occupations therapists, and family. This was especially the case when I was learning to dive. I spent hours and hours jumping off the board in an attempt to master my dive getting frequent encouragement from my parents. Some of the dives I made weren't really dives but rather belly flops that made my stomach look like a shiny read cherry at times. This, however, made me all the more determined to dive correctly. What a relief it was for me to hear my mom and dad comment as I leaped into the pool "Nice dive, George!"

Learning and developing an appreciation for learning from mentors and role models is like building a tower. I want to place a stone one over the other with every bit of knowledge that I learn to build my skyscraper of success. I will never learn all there is to know in the world but that's all right. Knowing the practicality of learning will be my success when it comes to seeing the big picture of life. *"Let the wise hear and increase in learning, and the one who understands obtains guidance."* (Proverbs 1:5)

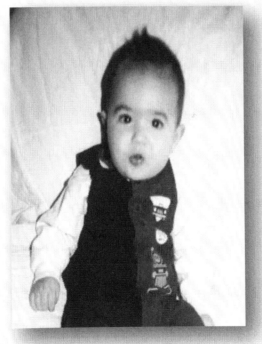

As a baby, I could only grab toys with my left hand.

After years of strengthening my right hand and leg,
I participated in a mini-triathlon,
running a 7-minute-mile.

Chapter 12 - Releasing Fears
of Peer Pressure

One day, I looked into the mirror and stared at my scrawny, weak frame. My right arm was smaller than my left arm. My right leg was smaller than my left leg. My chest appeared sunken in with no muscle tone. "I wonder what other people think of how misshapen I am?" I thought sadly to myself. Most guys my age were strong and athletic. They could run with ease; toss the football without effort; and kick a soccer ball with agility. I came to the conclusion that if I didn't work at getting stronger, the result would be a weak body. By watching athletic peers, I was motivated to work harder. This was good peer pressure for me, because it motivated me. I then came to the conclusion that my frame needed to change. I needed to bulk up a bit. That's when I started weight lifting, running, and swimming. This peer pressured caused me to want to be stronger. However, not all my peer pressure was positive.

I also noticed, as I grew older, that I was becoming more and more influenced by a dominant peer group. I realized that I wanted to do things in line with that salient group by copying their habits and beliefs. I realized that this was a good thing only as long as this peer group had good character traits. My parents strove to eliminate any bad peer groups by including me in healthy extracurricular activities. I thus didn't have the time to hang out with negative people who could potentially influence me to participate in things such as smoking, drugs, and sex. My dad shared his story with me about his early influences. While in his teens, he made friends with boys getting into trouble and the result was my dad getting in trouble at school quite often. My dad's life changed one late afternoon when he was staying after school as a consequence for his foolishness. The librarian, who my dad didn't know very well, stated very matter-of-factly, "The friends you hang out with will influence your life for good or for bad." Those words hit hard for my dad and he turned his life around, leaving his friends behind and began studying. Today, he is a successful software developer with two patents. I wonder where my dad would be if that librarian did not say those words to my dad. *"The trouble is not in dying for a friend, but in finding a friend worth dying for."* (Mark Twain)

As I got older, I began to feel more peer pressure. I felt like I had to do something in order to fit in with the rest of my friends, because I thought that I was a social outcast. I needed to realize the potential danger of peer pressure. According to the *National Household Survey on Drug Use and Health* from the U.S. Department of Health and Human Services, 74.3% of high school students have tried alcohol due to peer pressure. 3.1 million teenagers smoke, according to the American Lung Association. In addition, the Kaiser Foundation reports that about 50% of teenagers feel pressured with regard to sex in relationships. I needed to learn that if I let peer pressure govern my life, I would be more prone to things like: sex, drugs and alcohol.

As my dad pointed out, I will be a reflection of the friends I hang out with. If I would decide to hang out with people who like to party and get drunk on the weekends, then I would risk partying also. If I hang out with people who have good values, than I won't be as tempted to participate in worldly events. *"A friend is one that knows you as you are, understands where you have been, accepts what you have become, and still, gently allows you to grow."* (William Shakespeare)

I sometimes encounter peers who do not want to study or even think about their future. I am not going to ignore them but I will probably not have much in common with them since I have set goals I want to achieve in life. *"You're going to come across people in your life who will say all the right words at all the right times. But in the end, it's always their actions you should judge them by. It's actions, not words, that matter."* (Nicholas Sparks, American author and screenwriter)

According to an article in *Human Diseases and Conditions*: "A person influenced by peer pressure depends on many factors. People are less likely to be heavily influenced by their friends and more likely to make their own decisions if they have: high self-esteem; goals and a positive outlook on the future; good social skills; the ability to interact with people from many different backgrounds; strong connections to family and community.

People are more likely to be heavily influenced by their peers and less likely to make decisions for themselves if they: have low self-esteem, are experiencing problems in their family, such as divorce, alcoholism, drug addiction, or unemployment; come from families where there is little support or communication; strongly identify with only one ethnic group; feel distant from school and community activities; are afraid of not belonging or fitting in."

I am blessed to have a family that loves and supports me. I am also surrounded by a lot of friends, family, and teachers that encourage me to succeed. I knew that I needed to stay with friends who will help me grow spiritually and help me "keep my eye on the future." "*Iron sharpens iron, and one man sharpens another.*" (Proverbs 27:17)

Over time, I learned that I don't have to feel left out or depressed because I am different. Although I am not athletic like some friends, I am learning statistics and facts about professional athletes and sports so I can have a fun conversation with friends interested in football, basketball, and soccer. I realize my weak body, became a strength in my education. When others were kicking the soccer ball and playing on football leagues, I was reading piles of library books. I believe God is directing me in the path of education and medicine. Perhaps if I had excelled in a sport, I would have a different direction and would not have written this book. I have a friend, Caleb Prejean, who is an amazing athlete in football, soccer, and basketball. I believe God may be directing him to be a Christian athlete who will be a role model to many. Everyone has a great purpose in life. Just ask God, and He will direct you. "*Thy word is a lamp unto my feat and a light unto my way.*" (Psalm 119:105)

People who don't follow the crowd are destined to accomplish great things. People like Steve Jobs and Bill Gates are examples of thinking outside the box to create innovative technology instead of getting trapped into peer pressure. "*Without deviation from the norm, progress is not possible.*"(Frank Zappa, American composer and songwriter, 1940-93) People who strive to follow their passions instead of the crowd are the people who produce cool technology, great books, and become successful leaders. "*Whenever you find yourself on the side of the majority, it is time to pause and reflect."* (Mark Twain)

Thomas Edison was said to have a learning disorder, yet he went on to secure 1,083 patents! *"If you truly expect to realize your dreams, abandon the need for blanket approval. If conforming to everyone's expectations is the number one goal, you have sacrificed your uniqueness, and therefore your excellence."* (Hope Solo, American soccer goalkeeper and Olympic medalist)

One wouldn't think of spiritual leaders as being innovators, but many have paved the way to a new way of thinking. Jesus Christ, second person of the Trinity changed the thinking of thousands of generations with the greatest commandment, *"Love God with your whole heart and mind and love your neighbor as yourself."*

George graduates from the Valley Forge Montessori.

Mother Teresa did not follow the crowd when she began helping the poor in Calcutta, India. She faced many challenges and started out with hardly any money and really no place to live or to treat the dying. Mother Teresa had no place to put the dying people she wanted to care for; she had to beg. Mother Teresa was not trained to deal with diseases, and simply dealing with various illnesses - and the dying - was very challenging. Mother Teresa had all the cards stacked against her. At the time of her death, Mother Teresa's Missionaries of Charity had over 4,000 sisters; an associated brotherhood of 300 members, and over 100,000 laid volunteers, operating 610 missions in 123 countries. These included hospices and homes for people with HIV/AIDS, leprosy and tuberculosis, soup kitchens, children's and family counseling programs, personal helpers, orphanages, and schools.

Just recently, my friend, Matthew Holland, decided to think outside the box and left Louisiana to become a missionary at the age of 18. Just when teens are gearing up for parties, Matthew is gearing up to preach the gospel.

Having goals helped me to stay focus and not fall into peer pressure. Having goals makes it easier for me to see which friends have a negative influence on me and vice versa. I also use visualization to turn my attention away from negative peer pressure and achieve my goals. Apostles and saints have used visualization to aid in distracting their mind from the pain inflicted by those who persecuted them. They would be so absorbed in the love of God that they wouldn't feel pain. St. Stephen is an example of this, first seeing the heavens open up in the courthouse and then praying for his killers as they stoned him to death. According to an article on *stress-relief-tools.com*, visualization can be beneficial in seven ways:

- Self-development and spiritual growth
- Relaxation
- Healing
- Pain management
- Distancing
- Success
- Diversion

Athletes use visualization to help them achieve success in sports and maintain determination in the middle of negative peer pressure. For example, Jack Nicklaus, who has won a record 18 professional majors and is considered the best golfer in history, described how he used visualization extensively to help him prepare and win at golf. Nicklaus believed himself to be a successful at golf even before the game began. I want to do the same so my game doesn't end with the pressures of peer pressure. *"As you think in your heart, so you shall be."* (Proverbs 23:7)

Physically, I have used visualization to my success in karate. I would close my eyes and see myself moving across the dojo floor swinging my hands and feet in line with the exercise. Karate involves quite a bit of memorization so for me, visualization helped if I didn't have the opportunity to act it out. Visualization also helped to keep the memories fresh and associate practicality with the exercise. I definitely needed the practice and my sensei, Sensei Kelly Rhodes, at Acadiana Karate, expended much effort making sure that I understood my drills and made sure that I worked my hardest. Sensei Kelly stressed the importance of practice to further improve my drills and when I wanted to give up she inspired me to keep going. Though some may have thought it impossible, I was able to successfully make my right hand and foot strong enough to defend myself thanks to visualization and the encouragement of my sensei at karate. Sensei Kelly is a great role model and I wouldn't have gotten stronger without her help.

I also use visualization as I work toward my goal of being a neurologist; I am praying and visualizing myself studying, getting good grades, and avoiding a reckless lifestyle.

I believe God made me for a great purpose and I will continue to pray and listen to Him for guidance on my future. With God's guidance, I am trying to "keep my eye on the future" by achieving long-term success spiritually and professionally using visualization and minimizing the influence of peer pressure. "*At any given point you can release your greatest self. Don't let anyone hold you back. Don't let anyone dilute you. Don't be peer pressured into being less than you are. People willing to dilute themselves for the sake of others is one of the great tragedies of our time. Stop letting others define and set the pace for your life. Get out there and be your best. Do your best. Live your best. Make every day count and you'll see how exponentially more exciting, thrilling, successful, happy and full your life will be.*" (Steve Maraboli – speaker, author and radio host of "Empowered Living")

Chapter 13 - Deflecting The Desire To Be Perfect

Perfection seemed to be all around me and many times, I didn't seem to fit into this perfect world filled with perfect people. Television commercials depicted the perfect physiques movie stars, and athletes performing swimming technique with perfect symmetry and running and jumping hurdles with ease. These movie stars and athletes have perfectly formed bodies with working arms, legs, and feet. In grade school, I had trouble throwing a basketball, running in games of tag, and climbing ladders on playground slides. I got discouraged and almost gave up because I couldn't keep up with the other kids and I watched them race ahead of me in utter dismay. My flaws didn't stop and later seemed to magnify because of acne outbursts when I reached my pre-teens. As my acne became worse and worse, so did my self-esteem. I became depressed as I noticed other people and celebrities with perfect faces and desperately wanted what they had

I wanted to be perfect and have the perfect body, perfect face, even the perfect teeth, which also seemed like a dead end road even with braces. I am scheduled for teeth surgery at age 18 due to improperly grown teeth! I used to grumble at God and say, "What were you thinking when you made me?" I was, at times, angry with God for making a mistake – and that mistake was me. During those depressed moments, my parent's voices would echo through my mind, "George, you are *'fearfully and wonderfully made in God's image.'*" My parents told me this daily, in addition to *"I can do ALL things through Christ who strengthens me."* Thankfully, my parents' voices were louder than the negative voices that tried to overtake my mind. According to an article on *personalexcellence.com*, there are six downsides to perfectionism:

- Low productivity
- Procrastination
- Myopia
- Stagnation of growth
- Poorer health and mental well-being
- Sub-optimal relationships

"Perfectionism, in psychology, is a personality disposition characterized by an individual striving for flawlessness and setting excessively high performance standards, accompanied by overly critical self-evaluations and concerns regarding others' evaluations."

"Hewitt and Gordon Flett of York University conducted a variety of studies to examine the relationship between the need to appear perfect (perfectionistic self-presentation) and suicide, including studies that include youth. They are also testing a model they developed, called the *Social Disconnection Model* (SDM) that links social disconnection with perfectionism and suicidal thoughts. One study looks specifically at the social disconnection markers of bullying and feelings of social helplessness or never being able to fit in. "Suicide rates are increasing among youth," says Hewitt, a registered clinical psychologist. "Fuelled by fears of rejection and abandonment as well as a strong need to belong, be approved of and cared for, individuals with perfectionism do whatever is required to get the acceptance they need. This difficult path is characterized by severe and routine self-criticism, retreat and disconnection from the world as well as frustration, anger, and depression."

Hewitt has worked with artists, entertainers, physicians, elite athletes and others who can become paralyzed by their perfectionism and suffer from writers' block and other aversion behaviors. Their sense of disconnection and alienation from others, the most feared state of the perfectionist, makes them vulnerable to suicide."

Instead of looking at reality, I was looking at television with people who appeared to be perfect but had a lot of makeup to look perfect. These people don't even represent reality! If I had looked around me, "I would have noticed many other teens with acne too. The sad truth is that acne affects 90% of teens. In fact, some statistics even suggest that 100% of adults will also suffer from acne at some point in their life as well.

Acne, in addition to taking a toll on teens' self-esteem and quality of life, can even lead to depression and psychological issues, according to a new review of studies in *MyHealthNewsDaily.com*. For example, in a study published last year in the *Journal of Cosmetic Dermatology* that was also conducted by Feldman, researchers found that depression is two to three times more prevalent in people with acne than people with clear skin. Women with acne were two times more likely to have depression than men with acne, the study also showed.

In my constant quest to be perfect, I would try to minimize differences between myself and other teenagers by mimicking their clothes and try to create the perfect body image. According to a study done by Albertini and Philips: "72% of participants reported that their BDD (Body Dysmorphic Disorder) symptoms caused severe or extreme and disabling distress, and 21% were so distraught they had attempted suicide." According to an article on *utsc.utoronto.ca,* low self-esteem can have many negative effects including:

- Healthy and dissatisfying relationships with friends and family member
- Impaired academic and job performance.
- Anxiety, stress, loneliness, and depression.
- Vulnerability to addictions: drugs, alcohol, smoking, gambling, and online addiction,
- Avoidance of social interaction and isolate oneself. Feelings of self-doubt and worthlessness that interfere with learning and working more effectively.
- Academic failure (low grades) due to lack of confidence (ex. Performing poorly on a single test makes one underestimate their abilities and prevents future attempts to improve their grades.

Those facts prove how dangerous a low-self-esteem can be and it's all centered around the problem of being different and not looking as good as the celebrities. *"Perfection' is man's ultimate illusion. It simply doesn't exist in the universe.... If you are a perfectionist, you are guaranteed to be a loser in whatever you do."* (David Burns, physicist at the department of Psychiatry at Stanford University and author)

When the scales fell from my eyes, I noticed that most people my age had acne and some sort of challenge, which may or may not be apparent. The challenge others face may not be a physical one like mine. It may be a learning challenge, medical issue, or a spiritual challenge. "Zoe Troxell-Whitman, an *Anne Ford & Allegra Ford Scholarship* finalist in 2011, faced multiple challenges as a result of her learning disability (LD). In addition to her academic struggles, she suffered from the pain of being bullied at school. Luckily, at a young age, Zoe decided that she would not let these hardships stop her from accomplishing her goals of college even when others thought it would be impossible. She is now completing her senior year in high school as one of the top students in my school, with the goal of studying at University of Puget Sound, pursing a Masters degree in geriatric physical therapy." Zoe's ability to overcome the goal of perfection, and to accept herself, gave her the confidence to succeed just as other people with learning abilities like: Walt Disney, Alexander Graham Bell, and Winston Churchill did. *"You are the only you God made... God made you and broke the mold."* (Max Lucado, Christian Author and speaker)

Perfectionism can also lead to "people pleasing". Even though I love to make others happy, I realize that it is far from productive because I would constantly be changing things to accommodate others. As a result, I would hardly get anything done and my well being could be threatened. "In high school, some teens go from trying to please their parents to trying to please their peers, explains Deveney Marshall, program director at New Leaf Academy of Oregon. Tween girls who strive to please others are more likely to find themselves in unsafe situations because they follow the crowd in order to be liked and accepted. They may experiment with drugs or engage in early sexual activity, even if they know their behavior is wrong and would rather say no. In short, their decisions are based almost exclusively on the opinions of their peers. In addition to those cons, there are others according to an article on *livestrong.com*, such as:

- Low self-esteem
- Loss of personal identity
- Loss of personal rights
- Being taken advantage of
- Loss of personal time
- Ineffectiveness in managing work

- Inability to direct or supervise others
- Inability to achieve personal goals
- Inability to take a leadership role
- Poor problem solving abilities
- Burnout on the job or at home
- Chronic state of being unappreciated

If left unaddressed, people pleasing follows teens into college and adulthood. Their friends continue to take advantage of them; they keep saying yes when they really mean no; and they underachieve professionally because they lack the confidence to take calculated risks. As a result, they may become resentful in their adult relationships and stuck in careers that are less than fulfilling."

For me, recognizing negative traits such as perfectionism and people pleasing, are not helpful in my future success. I need to not compare myself to others or try to make everyone around me happy. The key to my future is how God sees me and how I use the talents that God gave me. By thinking long term, I acknowledge the fact that the future will be different from the present. My acne will eventually diminish and my self–esteem will soar if I view myself through God's eyes not my own eyes. As a child of God, a co-heir to the throne, I am royalty just as a mighty prince. (Romans 8:17) God's viewpoint frees me from perfectionism and trying to please others. I only want to please God and with that in mind, my life decisions are easier to make.

Today as I look into the mirror, I still see acne but I see more. I see the inner me with my values and beliefs all made clear --like a diamond with impurities but luster still showing and light still reflecting. *"Better a diamond with a flaw than a pebble without."* (Confucius) If we give our diamond the opportunity to shine, it will blind our eyes to the imperfections of our body and the thoughts of others. *"Do not let your adorning be external—the braiding of hair and the putting on of gold jewelry, or the clothing you wear— but let your adorning be the hidden person of the heart with the imperishable beauty of a gentle and quiet spirit, which in God's sight is very precious."* (1 Peter 3:3-4)

"With God, all things are possible." - Matthew 19:26

Chapter 14 - Repelling Attraction to Distraction

Ever since my physical and health challenges began, I was faced with distractions that could have led to me failing to accomplish my goals. For example, my desire for junk food could have impeded my development of a healthy immune system. My fear of risks could have stopped me from overcoming challenges such as biking, swimming, and diving. As I entered the teen years, my distractions seemed to balloon with the introduction of girlfriends and the temptations of drugs and alcohol.

In the case of girlfriends, it seems like I am missing out at times. There dances and social events that seemed to require a date or it would not be the same. However, I realized that having a girlfriend could be a big distraction to my studies and my road to success. I tried using that fact to dissuade my strong emotions. I also saw a lot of drama involved with having a girlfriend as a teen; boys breaking up with girls, girls dumping boys and so on. I have been distracted by girls myself and have found the experience very dramatic..

As a pre-teen and when I turned 13, my parents required me to read Christian books on the current culture of dating. One influential book, *I Kissed Dating Goodbye*, by Joshua Harris pointed out the following negative aspects of dating such as:

- "Dating leads to intimacy, but not necessarily to commitment.
- Dating tends to skip the 'friendship' stage of a relationship.
- Dating often mistakes a physical relationship for love.
- Dating often isolates a couple from other vital relationships.
- Dating distracts young adults from their primary responsibility of preparing for the future.
- Dating can cause discontentment with God's gift of singleness.
- Dating creates an artificial environment for evaluating someone's character."

I sometimes felt alone, and as if I were the only one without a girlfriend, but my parents and the message from Christian books about waiting made sense. One guy even accused me of being selfish by not having a girlfriend, and that I was only thinking of myself. I told him that by waiting, I am thinking of my future wife. I am trying to work hard in school and achieve my goal of a doctor so I can take care of my future wife and children, if that is God's will. The ridicule of not having a girlfriend was difficult but I also witnessed the difficult pain of friends being dumped by their girlfriends. As I keep my "eye on the future," I want to remain pure for my future prospective wife. Although, I do not know whom God has chosen for me, I want to respect her now by not "playing the field". I want to save my purity for her and be able to tell her with enthusiasm that I passed the test of time. "*Flee from sexual immorality. Every other sin a person commits is outside the body, but the sexually immoral person sins against his own body.*" (2 Corinthians 6:18)

Sadly, our culture contradicts the belief of being able to remain pure. From television, billboards, musical lyrics, to magazines at the checkout counter, our culture promotes immodesty and a selfish lifestyle of using others for pleasure. According to an article on *guttmatcher.org*: "Thirteen percent of teens have had sex by age 15, and most have had initiate sex in their later teen years. By their 19th birthday, seven in 10 female and male teens have had intercourse at least once. Teen parents have a hard time finishing high school, going on to college, getting a good job, and getting married. Teen pregnancy rates are much higher in the United States than in other developed countries, and twice as high as in England and Wales or Canada, and eight times as high as in the Netherlands or Japan."

Life can also be a battle between the forces of good and evil and sometimes it can be hard to distinguish right from wrong. Evil things can take the appearance, of harmless things or even good things and hence trick someone into doing or accepting it. This was part of the communist plan outlined in the movie *Agenda* by Curtis Bowers for the takeover of America. "The documentary starts off with a quote from Joseph Stalin, "*America is like a healthy body and its resistance is threefold: its patriotism, its morality and its spiritual life. If we can undermine these three areas, America will collapse from within.*" I see the decline of morality, spiritual life, and patriotism and am tempted to decline myself. However, by remaining pure, I will build a strong spiritual life as well as help strengthen my country with good values.

For me, I am trying to not get distracted with a girlfriend at this time. I have seen friends become distracted and lose their focus in school and their future goals. Some have traded a goal designated by God for a short term, unfulfilling relationship. I am trying to resist the current culture of dating and am waiting on God's timing for a spouse. Although, I plan to wait on dating, I have lots of friends that are girls. I enjoy building friendships with girls and having great guy friends that encourage me in my Christian walk and help me with my education goals. It is normal to have crushes on girls and I have them from time to time, but I am trying to "keep my eye on my future" so I can take care of my future spouse.

In addition to immorality, I feel pressured and distracted by people trying to entice me with alcohol. Every gathering seems to have alcohol as its central guest. Since my parents have sheltered me, I haven't witnessed many parties, but when I hear friends talk about hangovers, hiding alcohol in their system, and driving under alcohols influence I'm not very impressed.

The distraction of alcohol is serious and can lead to alcoholism or even worse death due to drinking and driving.

According to the Department of Health of Human Resources: "More than half of adults have a close family member who has had alcoholism or is still dealing with alcoholism. Children of alcoholics are at high risk for developing problems with alcohol and other drugs; they often do poorly at school, live with pervasive tension and stress, have high levels of anxiety and depression and experience coping problems. Teenagers who drink heavily are more likely to cut class or skip school, perform poorly in school, take sexual risks, and commit suicide. Heavy drinking increases the likelihood of delinquent and violent behavior including running away from home, fighting, vandalizing property, stealing and getting arrested. Regarding drinking in the home, parents who drink and who have favorable attitudes about alcohol are more likely to encourage children to start drinking and to keep drinking."

Sadly, I have seen many early deaths due to alcohol. My uncle's friend was dared to drink a lot of hard liquor at a bachelor party. This guy passed out and then later died. My aunt's high school friend was driving to propose to his girlfriend and a drunk driver hit and killed him. Another aunt's friend's son drank vodka daily morning until night and died of liver cirrhosis at the age of 23. After hearing of the deaths of those people, I have become disgusted by alcohol and its abuse.

According to the Prairie View A & M Academy: "Alcohol is an addicting drug with 3.3 million young men and women under 20 who are frequent drinkers. Alcoholism in adolescents develops rapidly, with some teens becoming alcoholics within six months after taking their first drink. Nineteen out of 100 young people 12 to 17 years old are defined as having a serious drinking problem."

I learned at Drivers Ed that alcohol slows down certain bodily processes including our mental capabilities. Awareness and judgment are slowed down as a result and we drive with a reduced perception that increases our chances of a wreck. In our nation, according to the Federal Transportation Department: "There is an alcohol related fatality every thirty-one seconds and intoxicated drivers accounted for 24% of all fatalities in the US."

I am turned off to the temptation of alcohol because I realize that it has no benefit to a young person whatsoever. Teenage drinkers assume many risks such as potential harm to the organs and rate of growth. This was proved by a study by NIAAA (National Institute of Alcohol Abuse and Alcoholism) according to an article on *ehow.com*. "The NIAAA cautions that the consumption of alcohol during puberty and adolescence may upset the normal increase of the sex hormones testosterone and estrogen. This dampening of sex hormones may in turn impede the body's ability to produce other hormones and growth factors that contribute to the development of organs, bones and muscles. Thus, alcohol consumption may prevent a teen's body - including the reproductive system - from growing and developing normally." In addition to having no health benefit, drinking can lead to abuse of other substances such as drugs. According to the article from *dosomething.com*: "Youth who drink alcohol are 50 times more likely to use cocaine than young people who never drink alcohol.". So alcohol has the potential to damage organs, leads to other substance abuse and, while it can lead to other substance abuse, alcohol is a major youth killer in itself. According to the same article, "Alcohol kills 6.5 times more youth than all other illicit drugs combined." *"Wine is a mocker, strong drink a brawler, and whoever is led astray by it is not wise."*(Proverbs 20:1)

By avoiding alcohol and parties, I am avoiding distractions that could ruin my future and even kill me. I want to watch what I put into my body whether it is food or drink because my body is a temple of the Holy Spirit. *"Do you not know that your body is a temple of the Holy Spirit, who is in you, whom you have received from God? You are not your own."* (1 Corinthians 6:19)

In addition to alcohol, drugs can be a distraction. Popular opinion of drugs can cause confusion. Unfortunately, the opinion of drugs is currently disintegrating from one that denounces drugs to one that accepts drugs as beneficial and good. I once went to a seminar on the negatives of drugs and learned that a sample of cocaine the size of a fingernail would kill a person. Recently, marijuana has been introduced to society in Colorado as a recreational product. This is not good because marijuana has the ability to reduce the well being of society. According to an article on *drugabuse.gov*: "A recent study of marijuana users who began using in adolescence revealed a profound deficit in connections between brain areas responsible for learning and memory. And a large prospective study (following individuals over time) showed that people who began smoking marijuana heavily in their teens lost as much as 8 points in IQ between age 13 and age 38; importantly, the lost cognitive abilities were not restored in those who quit smoking marijuana as adults." Marijuana impacts other aspects of the body as well. According to an article on the *nytimes.com*, a few other health problems are:

- Blood-shot eyes
- Increased heart rate and blood pressure
- Bronchodilatation (widening of the airways)
- In some users, bronchial (airway) irritation leading to bronchoconstriction (narrowing of the airways) or bronchospasm

(airway spasms, leading to narrowing of the airways)
- Pharyngitis, sinusitis, bronchitis, and asthma in heavy users
- Possible serious effects on the immune system

Even synthetic versions of drugs can be dangerous. Demi Moore proved this to be true after her daughter called 911 due to a seizure which Demi suffered after she had smoked K2 spice. K2 spice is a currently legal incense product, which is a synthetic variation of marijuana. According to an article on *EtraTV.com*, citing the *Hunterdon Drug Awareness Program*: "These synthetic cannabinoids (a substance that acts much in the same way as opiates) have been associated with impaired driving incidents, attempted suicides, and emergency department visits, and have been linked to such adverse effects as increased anxiety, panic attacks, heart palpitations, respiratory complications, aggression, mood swings, altered perception and paranoia." It is not surprising that K2 spice has the impact that it does because of its relation to the opiates. Synthetic drugs, K2 spice included can be very addicting. In another article on *Washington.edu*, a synthetic drug's potential to become addicting is made clear: "The actual effects that cannabinoids have reflect the areas of the brain they interact with. Interactions tend to occur in our limbic system (the part of the brain that affects memory, cognition and psychomotor performance) and mesolimbic pathway (activity in this region is associated with feelings of reward) and are also widely distributed in areas of pain perception." Synthetic drugs like K2 spice may seem harmless and a less dangerous form of drugs like marijuana at first but behind the innocent veil lays a vicious monster waiting to be unleashed.

Unfortunately, drugs and alcohol are taken rather lightly and praised in today's music. According to an article on *Health.usnews.com*: "The average teenager listens to 2.4 hours of music a day and hears about 30,732 substance abuse references in music in the course of a year. From the same article: "About one third of the most popular songs of 2005 referred to substance abuse, according to a new analysis led by researchers at the University of Pittsburgh School of Medicine. They took on the task of counting because they were well aware of data showing that cigarette-smoking characters in movies tend to increase smoking among teenagers. This new study, published in the February

Archives of Pediatric and Adolescent Medicine, didn't look for cause and effect. But it does give a sobering portrayal of just what's pouring into kids' ears." The study found that there were 104.5 references to substance abuse in rap, 33.7 references in country music and fourteen in hip-hop."

The effects of drugs and alcohol on the singers who promote them are no different than anybody else. An older example, Elvis Presley, who was considered the king of rock, would have drugs shots just to help him get out of bed. He preferred to be sober and had no love for life or else he wouldn't have done what he did. The drugs he took were unnecessary and he ended up paying the consequences. One day, he was discovered dead from a drug overdose.

Drugs aren't just marketed to older people. Sadly, they're marketed to children and young people as well disguised as candy or some other innocent substance. For example, drug merchants disguise methamphetamine as a strawberry flavored candy to make it more appealing to children. Thankfully, our knowledge is developing and we know more about drugs then we did before. Still, new things continue to be produced and it takes time for the side effects to be observed. *"If you would understand anything, observe its beginning and its development"* (Aristotle) Rather than play with these new products, it is best for us to wait for information, and studies to be released about them. Unfortunately: "In 2008, 1.9 million youth age 12 to 17 abused prescription drugs," according to an article on *dosomething.org*. According to the same article: "By the 8th grade, 52% of adolescents have consumed alcohol, 41% have smoked cigarettes, and 20% have used marijuana." So the use of drugs isn't very rare; "Around 28% of teens know a friend or classmate who has used ecstasy, with 17% knowing more than one."

I am constantly trying to remain free of temptation from these things knowing what terrible things might happen if I get involved in them. I am always trying to "keep my eye on the future". It can be hard but I know that the long-term benefits far outweigh any short term ones. Not only can drugs and alcohol negatively impact my future, but drugs could also end my life. According to an article on *wikianswers.com*: "The majority of long-term, hard-core drug addicts are dying in their

40s and 50s. The latest studies show that the life expectancy of a drug addict is 15 to 20 years after they start being a drug addict. 'The average U.S. statistics say that one in 100 heroin addicts will have a fatal overdose per year." Alcohol reduces perception and as a result can make driving dangerous if not fatal. "Traffic crashes are the greatest single cause of death for all persons age 6–33. About 45% of these fatalities are alcohol-related crashes," according to the article from *dosomething.org*.

There are many challenges that I will have to face, and I can use the power of long term thinking to overcome them. I can envision my future resources and my future reward will be better than any brief satisfaction that drugs and alcohol provide. Things like girlfriends, boyfriends, sex, alcohol and drugs can be very distracting. However, by "keeping my eye on the future," all of these things will become irrelevant. There is a world of fun that I can and will have by minimizing my distractions. Activities such going to parties and drinking may seem fun at first but in the end, the participants will end up worse than before they participated. If I continue

After years of hard work, I competed in a mini-triathlon and built symmetry to my weakened right arm and leg.

visualizing the consequences, distractions can be avoided thus making the road to success easier and more peaceful. *"Commit your work to the Lord, and your plans will be established."* (Proverbs 16:3)

Chapter 15 - Confusion with Evolution

When I was young, I loved reading about history. History has helped me to see the benefits of the future as well as the negative. One positive lesson I learned from past generations is their trust in God. People have an increasing reliance on technology and doctors for their diagnosis and medicine. While this is good, at times, I see science denounce God as a fairy tale or put God in a box and say, "God can't do that." If my parents had trusted in my scientific evaluation instead of trusting in God, I wouldn't be doing anything that I'm doing today. After having my MRI at six months, one specialist said I would never play the piano or play ball. It appeared to be true as my right hand was in such a tight fist, my parents weren't even able to open my hand. I was able to keep my determination to succeed because both my parents and I had a positive outlook for the future contrary to the outlook of evolution. *"The best way to predict your future is to create it."* (Abraham Lincoln)

I don't know where I would be today if my parents and me didn't believe in God. I truly believe I would not have the strength and complete healing if my parents had trusted in my scientific evaluations and even if my parents and I had believed in evolution.

As described in an article on *ehow.com,* "Charles Darwin's theory of evolution states that all living things are related and share one common ancestor. The theory revolves around the central Darwinian idea of natural selection, which states that organisms that adapt and are best suited to their environment survive, and those that do not become extinct. During Darwin's time, it was largely believed within the scientific community that a divine creator put all species on Earth. Since the origination of that theory, belief in God has greatly declined. According to a 1996 survey of scientists, only 5% endorsed the creationist belief that God created humans 'pretty much in their present form at one time within the past 10,000 years.' The majority of today's scientists support the theory of evolution."

If I believed in Darwin's theory, I would have no desire to work hard because science was against me and my progression toward a normal life. Things looked hopeless on a scientific scale. I wasn't using my right hand as a baby. I didn't walk until I was almost 3 years old. I didn't talk until I was past 2 years old. All odds were against me. According to Darwin's theory, I appeared to be an "organism that couldn't adapt and was not best suited for its environment." If I had allowed this concept into my mind, I might have become depressed from the feeling of worthlessness.

"One of the most eminent evolutionists ever, Harvard paleontologist George Gaylord Simpson, taught that, "Man is the result of a purposeless and natural process that did not have him in mind" I can't help but see the connection of evolution and a popular belief, relativism, and what might have happened if I bought into the theory of evolution. I would have bought into the theory of evolution; I would have been depressed about my future. *Christian Apologetics and Research Ministry's* article contrasts relativism with Christianity. "In modern times, the espousal of moral relativism has been closely linked to the theory of evolution. The argument is, in the same way that humanity has evolved from lesser to greater biological organisms, the same process is in play in the area of morals and ethics. Therefore, all that can be ascertained at present (and forever) is that there is no absolute or fixed certainty in the area of morality. Moral relativism is a philosophy that asserts there is no global, absolute moral law that applies to all people, for all time, and in all places. Instead of an objective moral law, it espouses a qualified view where morals are concerned, especially in the areas of individual moral practice where personal and situational encounters supposedly dictate the correct moral position.

In contrast to evolution and relativism, God's image has been impressed upon humanity (Gen. 1:26-27) so that human beings instinctively know God's moral law and what is right and wrong (Rom. 2:14-15). People don't have to believe in God to know His moral law, but in denying Him, they lose the ability to ground an objective moral law in something that transcends the physical universe. Without that transcendent God, as Fyodor Dostoevsky, a Russian novelist and short story writer famously observed, everything is permissible." Rick Warren in his book *The Purpose Driven Life* outlines five of God's purposes for us:

- **We were planned for God's pleasure** - so your first purpose is to offer real worship.

- **We were formed for God's family** - so your second purpose is to enjoy real fellowship.

- **We were created to become like Christ,** - so your third purpose is to learn real discipleship.

- **We were shaped for serving God** - so your fourth purpose is to practice real ministry.

- **We were made for a mission** - so your fifth purpose is to live out real evangelism.

I see myself as a work of art created by God. I am a "co-heir to God's throne". If I would view myself as evolving from an ape, I would not have the confidence and courage to tackle the future. I see the scientific facts of creationism outweighing evolution. Areas of proof backing creationism include: the rock layers, and abundance of coal and oil.

The characteristics of the rock layers of the Grand Canyon do not support evolutionists. Instead, these rock layers support a belief in Creationism. Evolutionists claim that the earth is millions of years old while the creationists claim that the earth is only about 6,000 years old or so based on the historical readings from the Bible. The rock layers in the Grand Canyon prove that the earth is young. As Abraham Lincoln once said: *"I can see how it might be possible for a man to look down upon the earth and be an atheist, but I cannot conceive how a man could look up into the heavens and say there is no God."*

Like a Creationist, I look to the Bible as my roadmap for life. Although some may consider the Bible to be outdated and antiquated, the principles are still relevant to my daily living. Many Bible verses encourage me when I become afraid such as, *"God did not give me a spirit of fear but of power and of love and of a sound mind."* (2 Timothy 1:7) This verse calms me when I worry: *"Be anxious for nothing but in all prayer and supplication let your requests be made known to Christ, then the peace of Christ which passes all understanding will guard your heart."* (Philippians 4:4-7) My favorite verse is Philippians 4:13 *"I can do ALL things through Christ who strengthens me"*. Other verses contain principles like abstaining from: lying cheating, selfishness, and procrastination. To illustrate these points, the Bible has stories and examples. These stories have personally aided me in my walk of life, giving me the inspiration to fight my challenges and never give up.

I find it interested that the Bible has a historical timeline with evidence to support not only the rock layers but the coal and oil as well. The Bible tells of Noah's flood that covered the entire earth in Genesis. Coal and oil were formed under great pressure so it seems to make sense that these substances formed when the water on earth reached to the height of Mount Everest. Genesis seven in the Bible indicates that the Flood covered all the hills and mountains on earth. This can be proved given the fact that ammonite fossils have been discovered in limestone beds within the Himalayas; the world's highest mountain range.

As a teen, I pondered the arguments for evolution and creationism. I looked at both points of view and see creationism winning time and time again.

Satan wants me to believe that I'm just a bunch of chemicals that formed out of nothing. Believing in evolution would be depressing to me, because I would not longer be unique but rather just another person in the world that needs to be provided for. The fact that one in six teens attempt suicide indicates that they might not be recognizing their uniqueness. According to an article on *crosswalk.com*: "Teens need to believe that life is meaningful and has a purpose. When teens feel that their lives are purposeful, they feel more capable and equipped." Today, I continue fighting to believe in my own uniqueness. I could have been depressed by evolutions message but I learned the truth. That truth is that God made me special and he loves me very much just as He loves you. *"In the same way, let your light shine before others, so that they may see your good works and give glory to your Father who is in heaven."* (Matthew 5:16)

Learning the art of fencing

Gaining wisdom from my great uncle at a family reunion

Chapter 16 - Never Cease to Keep Peace

When I was in grade school, I had a lot of tantrums. Some fits were due to sensory overload. For example, the wind, grass, sand, food textures, and even too many people caused me to scream and cry. My parents worked with me by exposing me to wind, grass, sand, food textures, and crowds instead of sheltering me. Eventually, I became calmer. However, I still cried when I didn't get my way. I knew when I screamed; my parents would get me whatever I wanted. It wasn't until my physical therapist in Philadelphia confronted my mother, that I stopped taking advantage of my parents concern. I was having one of my usual tantrums, when my therapist looked my mother, straight in the eye and said, "He's only going to get worse." My mother was horrified. She couldn't imagine me screaming any more than I already did. My mother asked her what to do and the therapist said I needed to be disciplined. My mother later admitted that she felt sorry for me due to my handicap and had a hard time disciplining me. With the boldness of that therapist, my life changed. At the time, I didn't think it was for the better, but it was.

A new season of discipline began in my home. I was given the 3-count rule to calm down or I would get a consequence such as a time-out, part of my allowance taken away, or grounding from a television show. My parents also instilled incentives such as an ice cream treats or a dollar toy at the end of the week if I did my chores and had a joyful attitude. My discipline didn't stop there though. I was slowly and carefully instructed to be a peacemaker with my sisters and friends my age. My parents taught me to seek the peace of Jesus within my heart: *"Peace I leave with you, my peace I give unto you: not as the world giveth, give I unto you. Let not your heart be troubled, neither let it be afraid."*(John 14:27)

Lessons on discipline and peace continued daily. I remember when I was at about 3 years old at the Valley Forge Kinder House Montessori. School was over and my mother was in line to pick me up. A teacher gently picked me up to help me in the car. I wanted to be independent so I started screaming. My mother said, "No screaming, George. You need to be polite. You need to be a peacemaker and just say 'No, thank you.'" I then started screaming, "No, thank you! No, thank you!"

I didn't quite understand the importance of being a peacemaker, but my parents demonstrated peace within their marriage and within our household. Yelling and screaming did not occur in our home. I grew up in a peaceful environment and saw how peace had the potential to influence others if I could maintain that peace within myself.

My parents also understood how effective a peaceful environment would be on my overall health, education, and strengthening of my body. My environment consisted of healthy food to heal, calming classical music to calm, scented candles to sooth, and encouraging words to motivate. I saw how the kind words and peaceful environment helped me to grow physically and spiritually. *"Kind words are like honey; sweet to the soul and healthy for the body."* (Proverbs 16:24)

The opposite of peace is stress. Unfortunately, stress is common in our busy society and stress can be deadly to our bodies. According to an article on *Mayo Clinic.com*, "The long-term activation of the stress-response system — and the subsequent overexposure to cortisol and other stress hormones — can disrupt almost all your body's processes. This puts you at increased risk of numerous health problems, including:

- "Heart disease
- Sleep problems
- Digestive problems
- Depression
- Obesity
- Memory impairment
- Worsening of skin conditions, such as eczema"

I am trying to maintain peace within my life with prayer, Bible reading, exercise, positive books, movies, and encouraging friends. There are just so many benefits! According to an article on *successconcious.com*, the presence of peace provides:

- "Better concentrations,
- Efficiency,

- A sense of inner strength,
- More patience,
- Tolerance, tact,
- Freedom from stress and anxiety,
- A sense of inner happiness,
- The ability to fall asleep faster.

"True peace can rarely be imposed from the outside; it must be born within and between communities through meetings and dialogue and then carried outward." (Jean Vanier, Canadian theologian)

My parents encourage me daily to maintain peace with my sisters and other people I encounter. My dad practices peace and humility at home and at his job. My dad is a great example to me in business, and his regular example helped me maintain peace while being yelled at on my job. On one occasion, while working my part-time trash job, I drove up to a restaurant in my golf cart and parked near the handicap parking. About five minutes later, an older man in a van pulled up and parked in the handicap. Even though I parked within the lines, his parking was crooked enough to bring his vehicle very close to mine. After he had pulled up, he rolled down the window and shouted to me to never park in the handicap. I felt like yelling back that I wasn't in the handicap parking, and he didn't know how to park, but I remember my parent's words: *"A kind word turns away wrath."* (Proverbs 15:1) Instead of shouting back, I apologized and moved my golf cart. The man calmed, "Be careful next time." I smiled and said, "Yes, sir." *"Without knowing the force of words, it is impossible to know more."* (Confucius)

Maintaining peace within myself is a strict discipline. It is easier to be cranky and snap at people. It is so hard for me to be calm when others are negative. Peace comes from God and in order to grow in my discipline of peace, I must grow spiritually. I do this by reading my Bible in the morning at night. I also attend mass on Sundays and other days if possible. I also spend time in prayer, talking to God and asking Him to direct me in my future and with my day. Throughout the day, I talk to God and ask for wisdom and give thanks for the many blessings. *"Peace is the fruit of love, a love that is also justice. But to grow in love requires work -- hard work. And it can bring pain because it implies loss -- loss of the certitudes, comforts, and hurts that shelter and define us."* (Jean Vanier, Canadian theologian)

Having a peaceful character will help me in college and in the business world. I have the choice to manage others with fear, anger and intimidation or I can nurture a work environment of success and peace where everyone wants to work. Current research in industrial psychology clearly shows that management by fear actually reduces employee performance. *"It is not enough to win a war; it is more important to organize the peace."* (Aristotle).

Whether it is making new friends or negotiating a business deal, maintaining peace with others is important to me. I sincerely believe that peace will make the difference between success and failure. *"The smile is civilization's finest adornment. It signifies the willpower and duty to fashion mankind's coexistence as quietly and agreeably as possible so that it will always appear friendly. For it is all a matter of appearance. The smile is culture's diploma: it is the diplomat's badge."* (Iwan Goll, author)

I want to create an atmosphere of peace today within my home and school. Maybe I can even bring peace around the world like Theodore Roosevelt. Roosevelt received the Nobel Peace Prize for his work towards a peace treaty between Japan and Russia. I liked that even tough Arnold Schwarzenegger saw the importance of peace when he said, *"You'll get more from being a peacemaker than a warrior."*

To maintain peace within myself, I like to pray this wonderful prayer of peace by Saint Francis of Assisi:

> *Lord, make me an instrument of your peace.*
> *Where there is hatred, let me sow love;*
> *where there is injury, pardon;*
> *where there is doubt, faith;*
> *where there is despair, hope;*
> *where there is darkness, light;*
> *and where there is sadness, joy.*

O Divine Master, grant that I may not so much seek
to be consoled as to console;
to be understood as to understand;
to be loved as to love.
For it is in giving that we receive;
it is in pardoning that we are pardoned;
and it is in dying that we are born to eternal life. Amen

I love my sisters.
They really help me remain peaceful.

Getting ready for a ride in the pasture

Chapter 17 - Never Neglect Respect

When I was little, I didn't want to listen to my parents. I wanted to do things my way. I did not respect their authority; this then filtered to my teachers and physical and occupational therapists. My disobedience and defiance at a young age was disrespectful and selfish. I don't know where I would be if my parents didn't take control by implementing strict discipline. In an earlier chapter, I wrote about the physical therapist telling my mother I would get worse if I wasn't disciplined. My mother had a hard time disciplining me when she saw how difficult it was for me to walk, use my right hand, and even talk. I can't even imagine how much worse I would be today if it hadn't been for that physical therapist in Philadelphia. At a young age, I didn't respect my parent's authority, or the authority of my therapists and teachers. That disrespect would have been like a weed with the potential to take over all areas of my life from government, employers, and even disrespect for the greatest authority, God.

Romans 13:1-3 says, "*Everyone must submit to governing authorities. For all authority comes from God, and those in positions of authority have been placed there by God.*"

My parents saw my behavior declining early on and knew that they needed to take action to get my tantrums to stop or I would not grow to be an independent, respected adult. I would become totally ineffective and unsuccessful in life because I would be used to having my own way

According to an article in the *Truth Magazine*, "Children who aren't taught obedience in the home usually have a hard time submitting to authority of any kind. Many parents, failing to recognize this, have absolutely ruined their children. Thus, we see children who run the home, disrupt the school, and take over the Bible class. Later in life, these children are a problem on the job, get into trouble with the law, and are a menace to society."

My parents sought wisdom from God and the Bible as they were trying to train me. They saw the importance of scripture in regard to disciplining me. "*Children obey your parents in the Lord*"; "*Honor thy father and thy mother*" (Ephesians. 6:1, 2) Children who hear the instruction of fathers and abide in the law of mothers find parents are "*fair garlands for their heads*" and "*pendants about their necks*" (Prov. 1:8, 9; 6:20).

Another resource my parents relied heavily on was from Dr. James Dobson's book, *The Strong Willed Child* and *Dare to Discipline*. In his book, Dobson encourages parents on how to properly raise their children with Christian advice. Dobson brought to light some important instructions helpful to my parents: "Two distinct messages must be conveyed to every child during his first forty-eight months: (1) "I love you more than you can possibly understand," and (2) "Because I love you I must teach you to obey me. When a parent loses the early confrontations with the child, the later conflicts become harder to win. We should make it clear to our children that the merciful God of love whom we serve is also a God of justice."

Although my parents took a firm stance with my tantrums and disrespect, they always said, "No matter what, we will always love you." I also see God's justice in my parents when they would tell me again and again, "We forgive you, George," after apologizing for such offenses as outbursts again and again. My parent's firmness was shrouded in love as they daily told me, "George, God has huge plans for you." During those years of molding and training, I always felt love in my parent's discipline.

As I grew, I continued with the respectful habits my parents instilled in me like good manners; greeting adults and others by looking them in the eye; shaking hands when introduced or when our in public; practicing humility and thinking of others; opening doors for women and the elderly; helping to clear a table or clean after a function.

As a 16-year-old teenager, I do feel disrespect on occasions toward my parents, but I have learned to think before I speak. My mother always told me, "George, you have two ears and one mouth. Listen more and talk less and when you talk; think about the words you are about to say."

One occasion when I really wanted to be disrespectful was when I turned 16. As a teenager, I wanted more freedom and independence. I was looking forward to getting my driver's license and had my learners permit at 15. As my birthday got closer, my parents had a discussion with me and said it would be prudent if we waited on getting my driver's license. At the time, I didn't have a job and we all went everywhere together. Getting a license, meant the insurance would increase a lot. I was very disappointed and wanted to yell and be disrespectful, but I tried to think before I spoke and worked on calming down. I later talked about my feelings of extreme disappointment. My parents listened to me and understood my view. They said they would pray about the right time to get a license and I decided they had my best interest at heart. I knew my parents loved me, and I trusted their decision, but I still couldn't help being disappointed. About two months later, I got a part-time job and needed to drive on the job and to the job. I was thrilled to get my license and my parents trusted me with my new freedom.

Disrespect seems to be part of our culture. I see disrespect on television, Internet, and commercials. According to an article on *familyschool.com*: "It is more difficult today to teach core values because of the influences of music, media, and the Internet in a teens life. For example, sitcoms teach them that being disrespectful is cool and funny. The commercials between the shows are no better. These commercials fuel their appetite for being self-centered and make them want the latest gadgets or toys. In a sense you are dealing with a society which teaches cruel behavior and selfishness and materialism."

Sometimes, it is difficult to be respectful to adults who haven't earned it or who are rude, but I realize the importance spiritually and for the benefit of my future success. I know that every time I am disrespectful, I have a sour feeling in my stomach as if I had consumed too much salad vinaigrette *"Without feelings of respect, what is there to distinguish men from beasts?"* (Confucius)

By treating people the right way, I will know how to make my business ventures profitable as well as those of my employers. *"I've learned that people will forget what you said, people will forget what you did, but people will never forget how you made them feel."* (Maya Angelou, American author and poet)

By being respectful, I also convey a good impression of my boss. For example, people view my work as a trash boy along with my personality and come up with a conclusion about the company that I work for. If people have a poor impression of me, they may have a poor impression of my boss and his company. That is why an attitude of respect is important. *"Pride must die in you, or nothing of heaven can live in you."* (Andrew Murray – South African teacher, writer and Christian pastor, 1828-1917)

The development of respect can also aid in other things such as creating better friendships with other people in general. I recently participated in a piano event, at which you perform certain piano exercises and play a song. When it was my turn, I went in, shook their hands, and played my songs. In between the performance, the judges and I were joking around and laughing. I was humorous as well as respectful which, in my opinion, was one of the reasons why I got a top score.

In another instance, I took a biology class a year or two ago and became friends with the teacher. We had a lot in common. My teacher was an ex-bodybuilder and I was still learning about the art of weightlifting so I asked for tips. Thanks to those similarities, we had quite a few interesting conversations. I worked hard at my studies but I also worked hard at being respectful. I believe that hard work and respect was beneficial to a good grade. If I hadn't been respectful to my teacher, I might not have gotten a good grade and most certainly wouldn't have established the friendship that I did.

Over the years, the power of respect becomes more and more clear. I am thankful my parents worked to teach me respect as a child. *"A child who is allowed to be disrespectful to his parents will not have true respect for anyone."* (Billy Graham)

Chapter 18 - Learning to Live
a Life Effective to Lead

On the night of the planned attack on Trenton by the Americans during the War for Independence, a terrible blizzard struck. The presence of the blizzard impaired vision and made the already dangerous mission even more dangerous. General George Washington was faced with the decision of whether or not to continue. "*A leader takes people where they want to go. A great leader takes people where they don't necessarily want to go, but ought to be.*" (Rosalynn Carter, wife of President Jimmy Carter)

As I struggled with my challenges, I was faced with the decision of whether or not to take charge of my future and make necessary changes in my life. I could take charge and make my future extremely bright or do the opposite. I decided to take charge and totally transform my life. Before I would have the ability to transform my life, I would have to make critical decisions though. When it comes to making decisions, I am hesitant and have a hard time deciding which road is right. Whenever I am undecided, I pray for God's guidance knowing that, even though I don't know the outcome, God does. Having the ability to make decisions is still a work in progress for me but I strongly desire to have the skill of decision-making. With that skill, I will be able to be a more effective leader. "*The greatest leader is not necessarily the one who does the greatest things. He is the one that gets the people to do the greatest things.*" (Ronald Reagan)

Leadership isn't just for the older adults though. As a teen, I realized that I lead everyday maybe not the same as a CEO's of a large corporation but I am leading by making decisions and setting a good example. As a teen, maybe you are the quarterback and leader of your football team, with people looking up to you for encouragement or advice. Currently, I'm practicing my leadership skills leading an American literature and ACT prep class on Thursdays. Since I received a good score on my ACT, I am helping others with the knowledge I acquired to get a good score. I want to assist in the success of others while working on my goals toward a successful career. In my classes, I am working on my speaking skills to articulate ideas and suggestions in a positive and encouraging way. We all have the ability to impact people lives for the better. Everyone has talents and skills that others can benefit others.

With my job, I am acquiring leadership skills by being on time; staying organized; articulating my conversation with intelligent conversation for improvement on the job; and encouraging others around me. My dad has always stressed the importance of being on time for a job or event. He said that if I am late, I am thinking of myself and not the other person who is expecting me to be there at a certain time. My dad said to be at least 10-15 minutes early for my job or event. This is hard sometimes because I like to take my time getting ready or savoring that tasty pizza before heading out the door. However, this shows responsibility and good work ethic that will help me with future jobs.

Working on the skill of communication is an important part of leadership. My dad always stressed the importance of using positive language, never slang or curse words. The language I use when talking with other people identifies who I am to them. I try to be positive and by keeping up with current events, I hope others will find my conversations interesting. I also try to focus the conversation on the other person and not merely myself and my interests. According to an article on *wiredtogrow.com*: "Part of being an educated person involves developing a well-honed vocabulary and a sharp mind—such that one can choose the right words at the right time in order to construct a cogent argument to influence another person (or other people) to accept/agree with their idea. Real leaders are not bullies. They don't shout at, beat down, demean, belittle, or embarrass their employees or direct reports—and that includes not using curse words directed at individuals. Real leaders bring out the best in their employees. They value them and their contributions. They don't demean their employees; they breathe life into them because leadership is all about creating leverage. And no one gets the best leverage from anyone else by tearing them down or mocking them or embarrassing them.

On the other hand: respecting the dignity of another person, helping them, encouraging them, believing in them, empowering them, drawing out the best that is in them—that is not only what real leaders do—it's also the best path to creating the best result. And since a leader's job is to create results through other people, there's no reason why you should ever curse in your workplace."

At home, school, and at my part-time job, I am working on the art of communication to be an effective leader as a teen and when I reach my career goals. To better prepare, I have read books on management and leadership by John Maxwell. One of his books, *Everyone Communicates, but Few Connect* helped me see the importance of building relationships and not just talk for the sake of talking.

As stated by John Maxwell, "When we fail to listen, we shut off much of our learning potential. You've probably heard the phrase *"seeing is believing."* Well, so is listening. Talk show host Larry King said, "I remind myself every morning that nothing I say this day will teach me anything. So, if I'm going to learn. I must do it by listening." A Cherokee proverb says, *"Listen to the whispers and you won't have to hear the screams."* Good leaders are attentive to small issues. They pay attention to their intuition. And they also pay close attention to what isn't being said. That requires more than just good listening skills. It requires a good understanding of people, and it also means being secure enough to ask for honest communication from others and to not become defensive when receiving it. To be an effective leader, you need to let others tell you what you need to hear, not necessarily what you want to hear. Gordon Bethune, former CEO of Continental Airlines, took this idea a step further when he advised, "Make sure you only hire people who will be willing to kick the door open if you lose direction and close it. You may be able to ignore somebody's opinion if you don't like it, but if the person has the data to back it up, your intellect should be able to overwhelm your vanity." A common fault that occurs in people as they gain more authority is impatience with those who work for them. Sometimes, I get exceedingly annoyed and irritated at people who don't understand what I'm talking about. I have the tendency to snap back an answer to a question and move on without really trying to understand the other person. Leaders like results. Unfortunately, that action orientation sometimes causes them to stop listening. But a deaf ear is the first symptom of a closed mind, and having a closed mind is a surefire way to hurt your leadership."

When it comes to communication, I need to be a good listener and really understand what others are saying. My mother would say to me over and over, "George, you have two ears and one mouth. That means you need to listen more and talk less." Listening almost a lost art but I am working on it. *"Everyone should be quick to listen, slow to speak and slow to become angry."* (James 1:19)

With leadership, I have the power to influence what others do or think. I want to create a positive future by influencing and challenging others to be the best they can be. *"If your actions inspire others to dream more, learn more, do more and become more, you are a leader."* (John Quincy Adams)

As I develop my leadership abilities, I must be careful not to let my pride get in the way because: *"Pride goeth before destruction, and a haughty spirit before a fall".* (Proverbs 16:18) This was definitely the case with Alexander the Great. Alexander the Great wanted to conquer the entire known world. He was a great warrior but as he won victory after victory he became more prideful. This is exemplified by the fact that he named more than three cities after himself. *"One's pride will bring him low, but he who is lowly in spirit will obtain honor."* (Proverbs 29:23) In the end, Alexander did not accomplish his dream of conquering the entire known world. His men eventually refused to go further out of homesickness. On the way home, Alexander died of an illness and his great empire crumbled shortly after that. As a young person working to become an effective leader, I realize my pride must always be in check. I must remain humble and obey rules from the people in authority over me. *"You plan a tower that will pierce the clouds? Lay first the foundation of humility."* (Saint Augustine of Hippo) The ability to obey rules is a must in the development of leadership skills. I know that I have to first be disciplined and follow the rules before I can be the one making them. *"Obey your leaders and submit to them, for they are keeping watch over your souls, as those who will have to give an account. Let them do this with joy and not with groaning, for that would be of no advantage to you."* (Hebrews 13:17)

As a young man, I am anxious to get out into the world and become the head of a business or hold an influential position in society. However, the teen years are a time for training, and I am trying to take advantage of the lessons. The desire to have authority at a young age without the wisdom of experience can be dangerous. For example, young King Josiah of Judah in the Bible ignored a prophet's advice to refrain from fighting the Egyptians. King Josiah, in a foolish attempt, tried to prevent them from crossing through Judah. The Egyptians were much stronger and crushed the opposition killing the king in the process. The king was young and didn't accept the advice of a much older counselor. By waiting to lead, when God's timing is right, I am ensuring my success. I don't want to obtain a leadership position and then have a bunch of problems because I wasn't prepared. I want to be ready and be able to answer problems or decisions that are thrown at me

In addition to watching my pride, I am also aware that I need to be responsible for the people who look up to me and set a good example. I know that even though I am not famous, people still watch my actions and even mimic them. I do the same thing as well looking at a person's actions not so much his words. When someone I respect does something, I immediately want to do what they do because they are such an inspiration in my life. What they say is not important to me as their actions are. That's why the old adage: *"do what I say and not what I do,"* is a pointless instruction. *"You need to remember the best legacy you can give your kids is an example of a life well lived. They may listen to what you say, but they will do what you do. If you tell them to take care of yourself but you don't do it yourself, what kind of message are you sending?"* (Brooke Castillo, weight loss coach) It really doesn't matter what we say when our actions speak the opposite. In all cases, our actions win over our words. *"Example is not the main thing in influencing others. It is the only thing."* (Albert Schweitzer, German and French theologian and physician, 1875-1965) I have learned that there are ten things that make a leader successful. According to an article on *Entrepeneur.com*, they are:

- Mission
- Vision
- Goal
- Competency

- A strong team
- Good communication skills
- Good interpersonal skills
- A "can do, get it done" attitude
- Inspiration
- Ambition

I continuously try to use and develop these qualities of a successful leader. It is a work in progress but I have learned many things.

I have learned that in order to be a good leader I must be a good follower. I have learned that the role of leader isn't easy, and I must be deserving of the position. I am "keeping my eye on the future" by practicing and honing my leadership skills. As an adult, I can then proceed to use those skills to my success making decisions and creating a peaceful and productive environment for others and myself as well.

As the snow swirled down on the night of the attack on Trenton, General Washington made the decision to move ahead with the plan of attack. The men under him knew the risks, yet they agreed to take them, believing that if their leader thought it was possible then it was. *"The key to every man is his thought. Sturdy and defying though he look, he has a helm which he obeys, which is the idea after which all his facts are classified. He can only be reformed by showing him a new idea which commands his own."* (Ralph Emerson essayist and lecturer, 1803-1882) The men crossed the icy waters of the Delaware River and carried out a successful mission catching the enemy by surprise. They never thought that the Americans would attack given the weather and had spent the previous night partying. Washington had made the right decision. *"Real leadership is being the person others will gladly and confidently follow."* (John Maxwell)

Chapter 19 - Mundane Chores lead to a Prosperous Future

"You have to do your chores, school, and practice before you watch TV or play games," my mother reminded me daily growing up. Many days, I didn't want to unload the dishwasher, make my bed, set the table, or pick up my toys. Sometimes I pouted saying, "Why do I have to do all these boring chores!" but my mother insisted that I do my chores joyfully to earn treats at the end of the week and a small allowance. Initially, my mother had to remind me and even gave me consequences for not doing my chores, but eventually it became a habit and I didn't need reminding or even treats. Today, I get up and make my bed, unload the dishwasher, feed the dog, put my laundry away, practice the piano, mow the lawn, and complete my school, all because of good habits instilled at a young age. My parents always included me and my sisters in household chores at a young age and told us that we were a team.

"Statistics from an article *helium.com* show that: "More teens who have a better relationship with their family (Including working with them) are more successful in school and work life. Being a part of a family is an essential part of a teens life."

As a teen, I questioned chores and felt lazy, however I continued because I knew it might develop my work ethic. I try to be disciplined in my day, and I attribute that directly to chores. According to an article on *Germantown Avenue Parents*, chores help young people to:

- Understand the value of hard work
- Set patterns
- Value cleanliness
- Build self-esteem
- Build relationships

When I was young, my parents didn't understand the importance of chores and didn't think I was strong enough to do them. I had trouble eating my food, tying my shoes, and even changing my shirt. The simplest daily task was overwhelming to me but I needed to learn to be independent. When I was a child, I would cry and scream about everything and was very demanding. With the help of my Montessori teacher and physical and occupational therapists, my mom realized that, spoiling me wouldn't help me achieve my goals of a strong body. I needed constant pushing to make progress with my strength and flexibility.

My mom thought that, since I had physical challenges, I needed to be coddled and not pushed too hard. In actuality, and as my Montessori teacher pointed out, I needed to be pushed out of my comfort zone or I wouldn't have accomplished anything in life. I needed to have a reason to self improve and the implementation of chores and other work provided me with that reason. Accomplishing chores also gave me a sense of confidence that I can complete other tasks as well.

I feel blessed that my parents enrolled me in the Valley Forge Kinderhouse Montessori. I remember the relaxed atmosphere of learning in the quaint log cabin schools. The schools sat on a few acres where I could run and learn about the trees and flowers outside. The trees and flowers were arranged in such a fashion that they looked as if they had always grown in the area around the kinderhouse creating a very peaceful and tranquil climate

The Montessori environment encourages "Age appropriate practical life activities. The practical life areas such as organizing and cleaning activities lay the foundation for the introduction to school. Practical life activities such as sponging, moping, sweeping, dusting, polishing, pouring and other home activities connect the home with school. Montessori School teachers show these practical life activities in a calm, unhurried manner, they act as guides and do not interfere. The child develops confidence and personal independence. The goal of Montessori School practical life skills program is to assist the child in developing social skills, personal independence, and respect for self and others. The indirect aim is to develop the child's gross motor and fine motor skills. The practical life activities are unique, purposeful, and simplified to the child's capacity. The repetition of practical life activities brings in a high level of concentration, order, responsibility, independence, accomplishment and respect." I have found this to be true. When I engage in an activity that I know will be of use in the future, I concentrate more on mastering it.

The implementation of chores has also helped me develop my work ethic. It taught me the importance of work and the potential rewards as well. My parents gave me an allowance after successfully completing my chores joyfully at the end of the week. Each week, my dad would ask me if I did my chores and if I did, I would receive a couple dollars. If I didn't, I wouldn't get any allowance. The allowance part was also important because it attributed a consequence for not doing my chores and thus encouraged me to develop my work ethic by doing my chores. My dad would remind me of the following verse showing the importance of hard work: *"Go to the ant, you sluggard; consider its ways and be wise! It has no commander, no overseer or ruler, yet it stores its provisions in summer and gathers its food at harvest."*(Proverbs 6:6-8)

Sometimes, I would get frustrated when my parents would say that I had to do my chores before watching TV or playing my video games, thinking that they were unfair. However, when I "kept my eye on the future," I discovered that my parents were looking out for my well being. It was a form of tough love. They knew that if I didn't do my chores than not only might my work ethic suffer in the future, but my physical well-being and independence in my future.

My mom teases me and says, "Your future wife will thank me someday because you are such a huge help around the house." My dad never relied on my mother to clean, cook, wash clothes, etc. He jumped in and considered it teamwork not one person's job even though my mother worked at home. The example of my parents teamwork created a peaceful, organized home filled with love and joy. My parents always say, "It's not a 50/50 marriage. It is a marriage where we both give 100%."

"Dr. John Gottman at the University of Washington studied men who did housework and child care. He discovered that men who do housework are not only happier in their marriages, but also have lower heart rates, and are healthier. In addition, the men who pitched in with household chores were less stressed and physically healthier in the four years following the initial research meeting."

As I go on to college, I see how my chores helped me develop good study habits and consistency in my routine that keeps me rested and focused. I continue to look for ways to improve my work habits for future jobs and to implement in my part time job. I like the five suggestions to improve work habits in an article on *career-success-for-newbies.com:*

1. **"Volunteer For Assignments** - One of the best ways to signal that you are a keen learner and are not afraid of hard work is to volunteer for assignments. Especially assignments that no one seems interested to do. However, do remember one thing. Under promise and over deliver on the assignment you volunteered. Do not be too confident that you turn a perfect opportunity into mess. Once you start the project, see it till the end. You would be seen as someone who is courageous enough to take on additional assignments. You would also be seen as someone who follows through in your work. This is the first habit you need to internalize.

2. **Be Nice To People** - I am sure we have all heard this often enough, to be nice to people regardless of their rank and designation. It sounds philosophical but when you are nice to people, they go out of their way to help you. And being new in an organization you would never know what sort of help you would need. Colleagues often like to work with nice talented people. When you have this effective work habit you increase the chances of people wanting you to work on their team.

Being nice to people is just common courtesy. There is nothing extra ordinary about this particular habit that you need special skills. A smile in the morning and a "Good morning" is a good start. In this day and age, people working in pressurized environments often use stress as an excuse when they blow up. Is this necessary? Nice is often reciprocated by nice. In fact, it can lower your stress level.

3. **Prioritize Your Work** - We all love to start work on things that are close to our hearts. However, often these may not be the most urgent and important in our list of tasks in the workplace. When you select

things you are more interested in rather than work that is more important or urgent, you lower your chances of success.

Have a list of things to do according to its strategic importance to your company. Know your role in completing the tasks at hand in order to achieve that corporate goal. When you prioritize your work, you are more productive and that increases your chances of career success.

4. Stay Positive - You have new people to deal with and people in the working world who behave very differently from school. It takes a lot of getting used to. There will be office politics to deal with regardless of how little.

Be above all these and stay positive in the face of challenges. When you are positive you remain focused on your goals. You make better decisions and therefore become more productive.

5. Highlight A Problem But Bring Solutions - The last effective work habit of the five effective work habits is to bring solutions each time you highlight a problem to your boss or management. You need to remember that when you bring problems and not solutions, it is often construed as complaining.

To avoid that label, offer solutions. A range of possible solutions also indicates to your boss that you have thought this through before approaching him/her with a problem. Have in mind a recommended solution amongst those you suggested.

I use the above methods to strengthen my work ethic as well as doing my chores. Having a work ethic is a very important component to future successes and, even though I didn't appreciate them at times, I came to see the value associated with chores. Today, I can look back at my parents insistent on chores and thank them for what they did. My parents knew what I needed to succeed in life. As Jim Rohn, a business entrepreneur and author once said: *"Discipline is the bridge between goals and accomplishments."*

My sister, Emily, and I play duets at the Christmas concert at Acadian Village.

Chapter 20 - Golden Road to Financial Success

From an early age, I had a fascination with money. I would put every penny I could into my piggy bank and used pennies, nickels, and dimes when I was practicing my addition and subtraction. My parents noticed this fascination and used it as an incentive for me to develop myself physically. My parents motivated me to ride my bike and dive off the diving board with a twenty-dollar incentive. As I got older, I wanted to learn everything I could about becoming financially successful. I've discovered that there are five key tips to financial success. According to an article on *rodgers-associates.com* they are:

- Live within your means
- Save regularly
- Eliminate the use of debt
- Invest regularly
- Maintain a financial plan

To me the most important one on the list is to save regularly and be frugal. Without saving and frugality I would end up living paycheck to paycheck.

Frugality seemed to be built in to me early also but there are times when I spend my money on things I later regretted. Some of my regrets include buying videos games I hardly ever played or a boring book that I put on the shelf and never read again. When it comes to making purchases I tend to think either short or long term. If I think short term, I tend to not pay attention to what I buy and how it affects my future finances. For example, I intend to buy my own car in a few years and am saving up to do so. If I spend my money now, I might not have enough to make my purchase five years from now. However, by continually developing the habit of saving, I will have more than enough when the time comes. *"Without frugality none can be rich, and with it very few would be poor."* (Samuel Johnson, English literature writer)

Saving can be extreme and needs to be balanced like everything else. In the extreme instances, some people watch the price of every little thing and never spend any money. I read a story once about a woman, Hetty Green, who lived over a hundred years ago. This woman had invested her money in the stock market and had become very wealthy and making over 100 million dollars in her career. Although, she was worth millions, Hetty would go to her office everyday to count her money dressed in rags. Hetty would never clean her clothes, not even her underwear because it cost money to have them washed. It's not surprising that she came to be known as "The Witch of Wall Street". One sad story was about her son's leg infection. The cost of the treatment was $150, and this was too steep for the millionaire. Hetty never had it treated and several years later, her son's leg had to be amputated due to the severe infection. I want to be wise with my money, but as my father always tells me, "People are more important than money." I want to always put people first and money is just a result of using my talents to glorify God. *"The love of money is the root of all evil."* (2 Timothy 6:10)

I am trying to learn how to properly save and invest so I can be successful in handling my finances for my future family if God directs me to marry. *"Frugality is founded on the principal that all riches have limits."* (Edmund Burke, Irish statesman, orator, and author, 1729-97) Logan Heley states in his article, *Investment for Teens*: "Teens with a steady income, no matter what size, should consider setting goals for saving their money or investing it." Even if you feel like it's an insignificant amount, you could be surprised. Putting your summer job money in a Roth IRA and letting it sit until retirement can set you up quite well. Two-thousand dollars put in a Roth IRA every summer can yield over $1.1 million at retirement."

My parents continuously give me lessons on saving and spending. When I was in grade school, my parents bought me a coin bank with three slots – one for spending; one for saving; and one for tithing. I was given a small allowance each week for my chores and then I first put 10% in the tithing bank for church on Sunday; 40% for saving; and 50% for spending. I was learning early on that I could save up for a big toy if I were patient. It also stopped me from screaming for a toy at the store. My mother reminded me I could get it if I saved up. My parents even gave me extra credit reading assignments or chores around the house to earn extra money. The most important lesson early on, however, was tithing and the importance of giving to God first.

My parents also taught me the importance of using cash versus credit cards. A credit card can be good in an emergency but it can be tempting to overspend and then have additional high interests to pay later. A Sallie Mae survey showed that the average undergrad carries $3,173 in credit card debt, the highest since the study began. The average senior will graduate with $4,100 in credit card debt, up 41% from the same study conducted in 2004. A Charles Schwab survey on teens and money reported that only 45% of teens knew how to use a credit card, while just 26% understood credit-card interest and fees.

Dave Ramsey warns of credit cards for teens: "Over 80% of graduating college seniors have credit card debt before they even have a job! The credit card marketers have done such a thorough job that a credit card is seen as a rite of passage into adulthood. American teens view themselves as adults if they have a credit card, a cell phone and a driver's license. Sadly, none of these "accomplishments" are in any way associated with real adulthood."

Work ethic is extremely important to being successful financially. It, along with a good attitude, helps determine how successful you and I will be. The fact that about 90% of all millionaires are self-made proves this point. It's relieving to know that not all of the wealthy are older though. With a good attitude, I can do anything, and that includes becoming a millionaire at a young age. In fact, forget millionaire; try billionaire. Mark Zuckerberg became one in his later twenties! His wealth originated from one simple idea. That's how many of the wealthy people of the world acquired their money. Wealth is directly related to how much we contribute to the planet. The more we contribute the higher our potential for earnings.

Many teens think that it is an impossible goal to become wealthy. However, there are quite a few young millionaires. Fraser Doherty, for example, is the CEO of SuperJam. When he was about fourteen, he started making jam and selling it in his neighborhood. At the age of sixteen, he left school to focus full time on jam production. In 2011 he raked in $1.2 million in sales and is worth $2 million. An even better example is that of Farrah Gray. At the age of six, he started his business career by selling body lotion and when he was thirteen he started a business entitled Farr-Out-Food which raked in $1.5 million in food orders in one year making him a millionaire at fourteen.

"A penny saved is a penny earned." This statement by Ben Franklin shows how much can be accumulated by watching even where your pennies go. I have discovered that I can build up quite a sum if I just saved a little money each week and invested what I earned.

"About 40% of teens said they could budget themselves, but only one in three could read a bank statement, balance a checkbook and pay bills. And barely one in five had any inkling about how to invest. Ross Levin, a financial adviser in Edina, Minn., teaches his teenage daughters about budgeting by giving them a set amount of money each month for clothes, entertainment and other personal expenses. If the girls are with their parents and want to buy something but don't have the money, Levin says there's no prearranged deal allowing them to pay it back. "They have their money, they bring their money, they spend their money," Levin says, adding that the strict policy has been a lesson for the entire family. "It's a very different feeling when you're making the decision and doling out the dollars," he says. "We found them making choices they didn't make when we were the ATM."

I started my investing at a very young age having obtained a savings account, some stock and precious metals by the time I was eleven. In the case of the stock market, my dad taught me the basics of investing and researching the history of the company. He taught me how to look at the earnings of the company as well as the price history. He showed me how to look at current events to predict fluctuations in the market. My neighbor taught me to research the character of the CEO and President and analyze if they were Christians and had Christian involvement. I always think long term in in the stock market, however I was able to double my money on the first purchase getting $200 for the $100 I initially invested. As a minor, I am not able to invest my money on my own; my dad does it for me analyzing my decision beforehand to make sure it's a good one.

Another way to learn about the stock market is through stock market games on the Internet such as *www.weseed.com* and *www.markeywatch.com* in addition to board games such as "*Cashflow 101*" and "*Stock Rush Board Game*". The games show the basics on researching companies; buying and trading stocks; trends in the market; and building a successful portfolio. There are many resources on the stock market and investing.

The library and Internet are some of the best free resources to build knowledge in this area. Whenever I get confused about a financial problem I either run to the library or do a search on the Internet. The library is an especially enjoyable place for me. I know what to expect every time I walk through those sliding doors: a cool, quiet environment with the rustic smell of six foot wooden shelves filled to the brim with all kinds of books. At one point, when I was really interested in finances, I would spend hours browsing through the library or reading articles on the *Wall Street Journal*. Through my studies, I discovered many things about investing.

I have learned that the stock market is based on the presence of fear. Currently, there is a lot of fear in America and as a result the stock market isn't doing well. However, if I "keep my eye on the future," I realize that I'm young and there is a good chance that the stock market will go once again. There is a great potential to make money of the stock market if the right choices are made. Take Warren Buffett for example. He got a large part of his wealth as a stock market manager and his investments in companies such as Berkshire Hathaway. Currently, he is worth around 45 billion dollars.

The value of metals isn't based on that solely the factor of fear though. I learned that a metals value is based on supply and demand if I wanted to invest in metals. I also learned that the condition of the economy is a factor as well. The better the condition of the economy, the lower the price of the metal and vice versa. Recently, I was entertaining the thought of adding more silver to my collection of silver coins and bullion. As I thought about it though, I realized that since the economy is doing poorly the value of silver is high and may get higher. While it may get high, my chances of making a large profit were minimal. Keeping that thought in mind, I decided that I was going to wait on my investment. *"Successful investing is anticipating the anticipations of others."* (John Keynes, British economist)

Through the development of my saving habit, I realize that the solution for a debt problem is reducing the amount of spending I do. I make it a point to always have a positive cash flow by spending less than I bring in. If I am in that habit, then I won't be as likely to acquire debt. Developing the habit of budgeting will also aid me as I work to prevent debt. Organizing the various areas of my spending and selecting a certain amount to be spent in each area will minimize the likelihood of excessive spending. At first, learning about finances was a bit intimidating. There just seemed to be so many decisions to make I started learning from my parents, neighbors, and by reading financial books. I have found that Dave Ramsey has great books and wisdom for teens on saving and being financially successful: "A 2009 Capital One survey discovered that 50% of teens wished they knew more about personal finances. Whether you have never stepped foot in a bank or you are actively saving and investing for your future, all it takes is a little effort and a lot of patience to become confident in your financial decisions. One awesome thing that you can take advantage of is compound interest. It may sound like an intimidating term, but it really isn't once you know what it means. Here's a little secret: compound interest is a millionaire's best friend. *'It's really free money.'* Seriously, just check out this story of Ben and Arthur to understand the power of compound interest. Ben and Arthur were friends who grew up together. They both knew that they needed to start thinking about the future. At age 19, Ben decided to invest $2,000 every year for eight years. He picked investment funds that averaged a 12% interest rate. Then, at age 26, Ben stopped putting money into his investments. So he put a total of $16,000 into his investment funds. Now Arthur didn't start investing until age 27. Just like Ben, he put $2,000 into his investment funds every year until he turned 65. He got the same 12% interest rate as Ben, but he invested 23 more years than Ben did. So Arthur invested a total of $78,000 over 39 years.

When both Ben and Arthur turned 65, they decided to compare their investment accounts. Who do you think had more? Ben, with his total of $16,000 invested over eight years, or Arthur, who invested $78,000 over 39 years? Believe it or not, Ben came out ahead ... $700,000 ahead! Arthur had a total of $1,532,166, while Ben had a total of $2,288,996. How did he do it? Starting early is the key. He put in less money but started eight years earlier. That's compound interest for you! It turns $16,000 into almost $2.3 million! Since Ben invested earlier, the interest kicked in sooner. The trick is to start as soon as possible. A survey by Charles Schwab found that 24% of teens believe that since they are young, saving money isn't important. Looks like we just blew that theory out of the water! That same survey also discovered that only 22% of teens say they know how to invest money to make it grow.

Why not change that stat and learn how to become a smart investor with your money? Talk to your parents or teachers about how to open up a long-term investment account so you can become a millionaire, too. And remember, waiting just means you make less money in the end. So get moving!" *"Money is only a tool. It will take you wherever you wish, but it will not replace you as the driver."* (Ayn Rand, American-Russian novelist 1905-82)

Reciting George Washington's inauguration speech at a poetry recitation

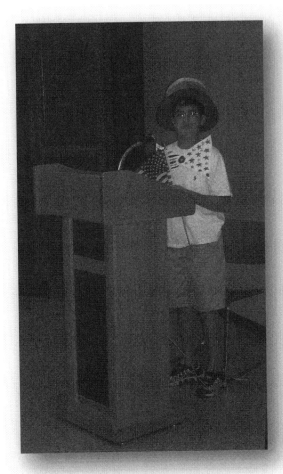

Reciting the Declaration
of Independence

Chapter 21 - Excelling in Appreciation

Sometimes, I didn't appreciate all of the things that my physical therapists, personal trainers, teachers, and parents did for me. There were many days when I was annoyed and even angry with others telling me what to do twenty four-seven. I was constantly corrected for not using my right hand. Regularly, I was reminded to straighten my right foot. I was even corrected daily to stand up straight. Some days I just wanted to yell, "Stop! I'm not working on this anymore," and tune everyone out. As a result, there were many days I was sullen and difficult. If I had maintained that attitude, I wouldn't have conquered the challenges I did. The thought of being "thankful" for others' encouragement did not even cross my mind. Without the help of teachers, therapists, my parents, and even my sisters, I may not be walking let alone running. I would not be talking with clarity. My right hand would probably be in a tight fist and I would not be using it to carry, push, pull, etc. I have so many people I am thankful for who helped me work hard so today I am strong enough to jog, swim, work, drive, and attend college. I wish early on that I would have had an appreciation but many times its after the hard work that I am thankful the people and challenging situations. It's just hard for me to recognize all the help people actually give during a trial. In the storms of my challenges it was hard to see anything for that matter including when the end is near. *"Giving thanks always for all things unto God and the Father in the name of our Lord Jesus Christ."* (Ephesians 5:20)

God tells me to give thanks in ALL things. It's easy to give thanks when life has no trials, but when challenges face me. I am called to give thanks. The people I meet throughout my life have caused me to appreciate even the smallest luxuries.

A few years ago, my family and I were traveling from Louisiana to visit family in Florida. We usually bring extra water bottles and McDonald's gift cards for the homeless we encounter. At one point, about halfway to our destination, dad announced we needed to pull off and get gas since the tank was low. As we were driving off the exit ramp, we saw two homeless men walking in the opposite direction. We quickly grabbed some water bottles and gift cards and met with the men at the gas station. My family and I got out of the car and gave them the water bottles and gift cards. The homeless men were very appreciative and told us their names were Robert and Dave. We also gave them some scripture tracts and told them we would pray for them. Dave said he would pray for us also. He then proceeded to tell us about his most prized possession in his backpack. "What is your most prized possession?" I asked. Dave grabbed out a book wrapped in cellophane and newspaper. He proceeded to unwrap it and showed us a small black Bible. "This is my most prized possession," Dave said smiling. Dave told us another story I will never forget. Dave said he had been sitting under a bridge reading his Bible when a man pulled up in a car. "Look at you," the man pointed. "God isn't blessing you." Dave replied, "Yes, God is blessing me." The man continued, "God is not blessing you. Look at you. You are homeless and sleeping under a bridge. God is not blessing you." Dave was not disturbed and said, "God has greatly blessed me. Look, God gave me the bridge to keep me out of the rain and keep me dry. God also gave me this bridge to sleep under. He has greatly blessed me."

I'll never forget Dave. He had nothing but a backpack and a Bible, yet he was so thankful to God. I want to have that kind of appreciation in every situation, every day. It's hard sometimes, though, because I have a downgraded sense of myself and get insecure as a teenager. I wonder whether my future is bright or dim and hope that I fit in to the teenage world at least a little bit.

According to the *Journal of Consumer Research*, the worse kids feel about themselves, the more obsessed they become with buying stuff. And because self-esteem takes a big hit during adolescence, countless retailers and brands are vying for the attention of teenagers trying to purchase their identity.

Author John Rosemond says that: "While adults generally attain 10% to 20% of the things they desire, kids are accustomed to receiving about 80% of what they want. And parents often make sure their teenagers aren't deprived of any luxury. No wonder materialism has such a strong hold on kids today.

The problem is that 'stuff' can't meet our deepest needs or heal our hurts. Only God, the giver of all good gifts, can do that. Being content with—and grateful for—what we have is rooted in this knowledge of the source of all our blessings."

There are times when I look longingly at other peoples' stuff with a somewhat materialistic attitude. When I catch myself doing this I try to distinguish the desire as either a need or a want. As a teenager, I especially have the tendency to have a materialistic attitude toward cars. It's hard for me to see a sports car and not want to drive it myself. In these instances I constantly remind myself of the pitfalls of materialism. If let loose the monster of materialism, it could completely ruin my life leaving me self-centered and broke in the end. Throughout history, there have been many examples of people who have fallen to materialism. Michael Jackson is perhaps the best example. At the time of his death, he was some $400 million in debt. This debt was accumulated from a wide range of expenses including: maintaining a ranch that featured: two railway lines, a fire department, two helicopter pads and theme park rides, his seventy-five cars, medical expenses of twenty-five thousand a month, and lavish gifts such as a $637,000 necklace purchased for a friend. Materialism can have a negative impact in a number of ways. In an article on *generalspeaking.com*, five downsides of materialism are outlined:

- High importance of money=low satisfaction with life
- Materialism is associated with mental health problems
- Materialistic goals can never be fulfilled
- Self-esteem isn't found in things
- Materialists live avoidance-based lives

In addition, materialism is associated with an increased likelihood of depression. According to an article on *Mail Online*: "A study of youngsters aged between nine and 12 found those who believed happiness was linked to money, fame and beauty were more likely to suffer depression. Among a group of 400 children, 16 reported levels of clinical depression while 112 were found to be vulnerable to depression in future, experts told the British Psychological Association's annual conference in Bournemouth.

The research, led by Dr. Helen Street from Queen Elizabeth Medical Centre in Western Australia, focused on children's beliefs about happiness and how these related to their goals in life. A significant relationship was identified between the children's understanding of happiness and their vulnerability to depression. Depressed children were more likely to believe that happiness was something achieved through the acquisition of money, fame and beauty. These children wanted to be rich and famous above all else in life. Happier children were more inclined to believe that feeling good was about healthy attitudes and the experience of pursuing goals, whatever the outcomes might be."

"Contentment is natural wealth, luxury is artificial poverty." (Socrates)

Sometimes I don't appreciate how God made me. At times, I am jealous of others with strong legs and strong arms. Then God places people in my path to realize the path to a thankful heart. One such person was Ray, an elderly, heavy-set man in a wheelchair with a colorful blanket over his paralyzed legs. Every Saturday morning, I would see Ray on the corner of a busy street; in Lafayette Louisiana sitting in his wheelchair with a small stand filled with rosaries. Ray would wheel down the street to the corner to sell his homemade rosaries. Even in the rain, Ray could be seen at his post with a large multicolored umbrella over him and a smaller one over his rosary stand. One day, my mother wanted to stop and buy a couple rosaries. Ray had a huge smile and was happy to make a sale. While my mom was paying Ray for the rosaries, I asked Ray why he was selling rosaries. Ray smiled and said, "I can still glorify God by selling my hand-made rosaries in retirement. I still can spread the gospel."

Ray had a thankful heart. Even though he was in his 80s, overweight, and in a wheelchair, he still had a purpose and was happy to serve God.

According to an article on *huffingtonpost.com*, there are ten benefits of gratitude.

- Linked to better mental health
- Boosts well-being
- Linked with better grades

- Makes you a better friend
- Helps you sleep better
- Strengthens relationships
- Benefits the heart
- Good for team morale
- Linked with better immune health
- Protects against negative emotions that come with a loss

Have you noticed those who have a 'brighter side of things' outlook tend to be happier? That's because thankfulness brings joy and gladness to our hearts. It helps eradicate worry and refreshes our souls with the peace of God."

I have learned that I don't have to be super rich and earn a lot of money to be happy. True happiness doesn't come from material acquisitions. It comes from me having the ability to enjoy and relish the small things in life. *"The secret of happiness, you see, is not found in seeking more, but in developing the capacity to enjoy less."* (Socrates) Buying things can make me happy only in the short term but in the long term I'll find myself wanting something newer or better. In short, the happiness obtained with purchases is a false happiness. *"It isn't what you have or who you are or where you are or what you are doing that makes you happy or unhappy. It is what you think about it."* (Dale Carnegie) So when I look at people go by in their sports cars and begin to think they're happy, I think again. They may or may not be happy it all depends on their level of contentment and appreciation. *"Do not spoil what you have by desiring what you have not."* (Ann Brashares, American writer of young adult fiction)

"A new study shows that a teen who learns to count his or her blessings can actually play an important role in positive mental health. As gratitude increases, so do life satisfaction, happiness, positive attitudes, hope and even academic performance." When I am ungrateful about something I have a tendency to become distracted from my schoolwork because my mind is focused like a laser beam on the thing I want.

Giacomo Bono, study author and a professor of psychology at California State University, Dominguez Hills, said it seems there's not much time these days for teens to pause and consider their appreciation of their friendships, activities they enjoy or even the food on the table.

But among those kids who say they feel grateful for a variety of things in their lives, Bono found an association with critical life skills such as cooperation, a sense of purpose, creativity and persistence."

I have so many things to be thankful for the list could stretch to the moon but I have to say that being an American is close to the top of the list. In America, I have the potential to achieve my goals. I also have so many possessions compared with the rest of the world. However, I still find myself wanting more and more and taking for granted the conveniences that I already have. Transportation is a good example. In fact, there's an average of one car for 85 people in China. In America, it is not unusual to see people with two, three, or four cars. As a whole, our nation is one of the wealthiest nations on the planet. Americans talk about their salaries in terms of thousands. Poor people in other countries such as Mexico do not even talk about their pay in the hundreds. In fact, some twenty million Mexicans live on about two dollars a day!

Unfortunately, amidst all my blessings it is hard to see the true plight of the world. It is hard to understand that some people four times less in a day than I earn in only one hour. It is hard to realize that Indian newborn deaths because of starvation total more than 900,000 babies a year which s is roughly 28% of the world's total newborn child loss. I live in a giant bubble world which seems like paradise to many people of this world and who would love to be in my place. The large majority of the time, I am thrilled to be here. Thrilled to live like a king eating and drinking when I want, being able to have many comforts and entertainment.

The fight to keep an attitude of gratitude is continuous. Sometimes, I take things for granted such as living in such a great country and having supportive people to encourage me and push me toward my goals. However, I have come to see how a materialistic and selfish attitude can have a negative impact my future plans and my spiritual growth. When I catch myself thinking in an unappreciative non-content way, I "keep my eye on the future" by listing everything I have to be thankful for. The list is so long it certainly could reach to the moon and beyond. *"Be grateful for what you have now. As you begin to think about all the things in your life you are grateful for, you will be amazed at the never-ending thoughts that come back to you of more things to be grateful for. You have to make a start, and then the law of attraction will receive those grateful thoughts and give you more just like them."* (Rhonda Byrne, Australian television writer and producer)

"Iron Sharpens Iron." -Proverbs 27:13
My family sharpens me.

Learning to fly with my Uncle Sheldon

Chapter 22 - The Knowledge Found in College

At five years old, I couldn't sit still in my desk. I needed to move. I needed to talk. I couldn't understand how the other students could sit so still and quiet. I wanted to scream and sometimes I did scream, which got me in trouble. When I did finally focus, it was on a topic such as history, but I wanted to know more. I wanted to keep learning. I didn't want to stop history and learn another subject. I wanted all the details. The classroom couldn't stop for me and wait for me. It was time for reading and I needed to stop learning about history. Transitions from subject to subject would make me cry and scream out of irritation and dismay. My parents realized the traditional classroom was not conducive to my learning style. I learned by talking and at times, I needed hours on a subject to learn all the details. I also required a lot of movement, which helped me retain information. A regular classroom did not allow for movement, which is distracting for other students. After much prayer, my parents decided to homeschool me from first grade until my recent early graduation. My learning style was so different when I was younger that I don't know if I would have even made it to graduation. My parents stressed the importance of a college education and continually encouraged me to develop my love of learning.

As a long-term benefit, the work environment is better and I have the potential to live comfortably. According to the Bureau of Labor Statistics, "Not only is there a $400 per week difference in earnings between those with a high school diploma and those with a bachelor's degree. There is also a substantial difference in unemployment. As of the end of 2011, high-school only workers were unemployed at a rate of 9.4% while those with a bachelor's degree had an unemployment rate of 4.9% (4.1% as of July 2012). Most interesting is the fact that the total cost of degree acquisition ($64,000) is repaid through the increased, salary ($1600 per month, or $19,200 per year) in less than four years. Not a bad ROI, and with a 50% increase in job security to boot. The difference between a degree holder's earnings and those of a high school-only worker are sizeable over a lifetime. According to the *U.S. Government Info* web site: " a high school graduate can expect, on average, to earn $1.2 million; those with a bachelor's degree $2.1 million; and people with a master's degree $2.5 million."

To prep for college, I had to take the ACT. I used tips such as getting plenty of sleep, exercise and good food from the *Official ACT Study Guide* and also took practice tests from the same book to prepare for the test. In addition, the public library offered practice tests and tips, which were very helpful. I was initially stressed out because I knew that colleges relied heavily on the ACT and SAT to determine college entrance. That was one of the reasons why I did so poorly on a practice test prior to taking the real thing. I decided that my fear of getting a bad score had to go and I spent many hours developing confidence about the test and developing a nonchalant attitude toward it. I would visualize myself, a muscular, brown-haired boy about five-foot-five inches tall casually walking into the building, taking a seat at my desk and finishing early with plenty of time to look over my answers. My efforts finally paid off and I ended up getting a 24 on the test. *"God did not give me a spirit of fear, but of power and of love and of sound mind."* (2 Timothy 1:7)

While my score was good, it wasn't perfect which was a good thing because it helped me not to become overconfident. I was then free to think more realistically about college and the implications of college. The whole concept of college is a bit freaky to me. There are just so many choices to make. There are many things like career choices to think about as well as what my professors would be like.

From an early age, my parents had impressed on me the importance of selecting a career that I loved. I saw the wisdom in this because if I had a job that I wasn't passionate about than I wouldn't be happy. *"Learning without reflection is a waste. Reflection without learning is dangerous."* (Confucius) I wanted to use my talents to glorify God so I prayed for direction and wisdom about my future. My parents also told me that it was all right to change my mind about my career even if I was almost complete with my college training. Their logic was that the extra years spent on studies would more than make up for the time spent at work. I am so grateful to have parents who are supportive about my career opinions even if it means changing my mind at the lasts minute. *"Choose a job you love, and you'll never have to work a day in your life"* (Confucius) By "keeping my eye on the future," I will master any future career! *"You have to be burning with "an idea, or a problem, or a wrong that you want to right." If you're not passionate enough from the start, you'll never stick it out."* (Steve Jobs)

Another preparation I made for college was preparing to be challenged in my Catholic Christian faith. The professors and other students at the university may test my faith, but with prayer I will be ready for any challenge. Recently, this happened to one of my friends. Her professor was very anti-Catholic and tried to flunk her because of her beliefs. My friend took a loving approach toward her teacher and engaged the teacher in friendly conversations. In the end, the professor had a respect for my friend and a better understanding of Christianity that he otherwise wouldn't have had.

Unfortunately, many teens are not grounded in their faith. The majority of Christian teens lose their faith after entering college. This is obvious proven by the fact that 62% of students entering college with some religious belief, leave without it.

According to an article on *worldoncampus.com*: "Christian students attending secular colleges face more than academic challenges. Secular campus life often causes them to wrestle with their beliefs, with many even walking away from faith before graduation. But those who minister on secular campuses say that with a little planning and a lot of prayer, students can survive school with an even stronger, more vibrant and personal faith. Displacement and peer pressure are not the only factors challenging students. Young Christians often find their faith challenged intellectually. On a secular campus, students are confronted with questions of science, religion, and the truthfulness of the Bible. Students should make and keep goals. Saying no to temptations and yes to other life choices is a must for students. Making commitments to good grades, good relationships, and involvement on campus are ways to clarify the college experience."

These facts, shouldn't, dissuade me from attending college and getting a degree. Some professors may discourage me from my faith but throughout my life I will be tempted to walk away from my faith.

Throughout college, I will remain in prayer, continue the daily habit of reading my Bible, and surround myself with good Christians. *"Be on your guard; stand firm in the faith; be men of courage; be strong."*(1 Corinthians 16:13)

College also has other minor challenges that scares me such as finding my classes and getting used to the environment. I have all new surroundings to get used to and I will eventually. I may even get lost but there are many other students I can ask for directions. I am fortunate the college I am attending is smaller than most. My dad printed out a map for me and will help me on my first day, but after that I am on my own.

However, it's all in perspective. For example, to someone who is writing a book for the first time, the task may seem very challenging if not impossible. However, someone who has written a book before usually has a different view. This view is basically the opposite of the inexperienced writer's. I can use perceptions to my advantage by creating the right viewpoint of a challenge. I cannot have a negative perception of that challenge, because it will be a barrier to our success. Instead, I need to think positive thoughts and create a positive perception. *"It is during our darkest moments that we must focus to see the light."* (Aristotle) This is what I did when I decided to write this book. I did have doubts about my ability to write such a book, but I didn't let those doubts take control. I was optimistic and had that accomplishing perception even though I hit walls. At times, I despaired that the book would ever be published. However, if I had instead maintained a negative doubting perception though, I might not have been able to finish the book. *"Always do what you are afraid to do."* (Ralph Emerson). I have discovered that there are 10 perception tools that I can use to succeed in both college and other ambitions. Following are tools explained in an article by Dr. Edward Bono from *debomoconsulting.com*:

"Tool 1 - Consequences and Sequels - Look ahead to see the consequences of an action, plan, decision, or rule.

Tool 2 - Plus, Minus, Interesting - Ensure that all sides of a matter have been considered before a decision or commitment is made.

Tool 3 - Recognize, Analyze, Divide - Break a larger concept into smaller, more manageable parts.

Tool 4 - Consider All Factors - Explore all factors related to an action, decision, plan, judgment, or conclusion.

Tool 5 - Aims, Goals, Objectives - Focus directly and deliberately on the intentions behind actions.

Tool 6 - Alternatives, Possibilities, and Choices - Deliberately try to find other ways.

Tool 7 - Other People's Views - Put yourself in others' shoes.

Tool 8 - Key Values Involved - Ensure that your thinking serves your values.

Tool 9 - First Important Priorities - Select the most important ideas, factors, objectives, consequences, etc.

Tool 10 - Design/Decision, Outcome, Channels, Action - Direct attention to the outcome of the thinking and action that follows."

If I use these tools and keep a positive perception of college I will succeed. I can't just live in fear because I won't accomplish anything in life. Theodore Roosevelt once said, *"Get action. Seize the moment. Man was never intended to be an oyster"*. With a positive, confident attitude, I can get action and seize the moment coming out of a shell of fear. Mistakes and problems may occur, and I may get lost going to a class or I may have a professor who is anti-Catholic but if I constantly live in fear with a negative perception of college, I'll never accomplish my dreams. *"Hold all thoughts captive to the Lord."* (2 Corinthians 10:5)

Throughout my life, my parents would sing me this Bible song, *"I can do all things through Christ who strengthens me."* (Philippians 4:13) This verse rings through my ears and sings through my heart filling my mind with the wisdom of God. I saw how Christ gave me strength to walk, talk, and use my right hand. I have seen the Holy Spirit help me swim, dive, and run a mini-triathlon. My heavenly Father strengthened my fingers to play the piano and healed my mind to get good scores for college. I know Jesus will walk with me next week to my first college class and guide my path to a future as a neurologist. *"You never fail until you stop trying."* (Albert Einstein)

Starting college at age 16

When my physical therapist told me that I was going to have to include more cardio, I knew there was hard work and pain ahead. My therapist noticed that small exercises strained me and made me out of breath. I had to admit, I was out of shape. My new jogging routine included painful jogging cramps and muscle strains that had me wincing as I ran. I remained respectful though and didn't yell at him even though I was more than a little stressed out. *"The greatest weapon against stress is our ability to choose one thought over another."* (William James, American philosopher and physiologist, 1840-1910)

Personally, every time I undergo some change, there is stress involved. It's hard for me to change because I'm cozy with my routine and am familiar with it. New routines require mental and physical exertion in order to adjust. However I have found that, in the long term, change is often for the better. Instituting a jogging routine, greatly aided my health even though it was a bit painful at first. As I jogged, the wind blew through my nostrils energizing me and the sun that beamed down on my head made me feel warm and happy inside. The crunching sound of the green grass under my shoes and the sun's emerald reflection on the pond's surface refreshed me. After jogging, I would arrive home feeling ready to tackle my many projects." *"A ship is safe in harbor, but that's not what ships are for."* (William Shedd, American theologian, 1820-94)

When I am faced with a change that is stressful, I find that it is always helpful to have a positive attitude. By thinking positively, I reduce the amount of stress associated with the change. *"Smile more. Don't take life too seriously and improve your ability to cope with stressful situations by seeing the funny side of whatever happens"* (Professor Richard Wiseman)

Stress isn't healthy at all but unfortunately, is very prevalent in society. "According to a 1996 survey conducted by *Prevention* magazine: "73% of Americans experience great stress on a weekly basis." Stress can have an impact on health hence having an impact on goal attainment. In a study by the American Physiological Association

"30% of tweens and 42% of teens say they get headaches" in 2009. This can lead to other things such as restlessness with "39% of tweens and 49% of teens report difficulty sleeping," from the same study. It's a chain reaction."

The impact of stress is explained in an article on *healingheartpower.com*: "Long-term stress (more than 15 minutes) increases the stress hormone cortisol. Cortisol makes us hyper-vigilant, and mobilized to cope with stress and emergencies. To cope with such emergencies, cortisol begins to break down non-essential organs and tissues to feed vital organs. When cortisol stays at high levels, it automatically digests bones, muscles and joints to obtain key nutrients to maintain the nervous system and vital internal organs. It also makes us hungry, causing us to reach for high calorie food." In short, Cortisol is associated with:

- Aggression
- Arousal
- Activates addictions
- Associated with depression
- Can be toxic to brain cells
- Breaks down muscles, joints and bones
- Weakens immune system
- Increases pain
- Clogs arteries, promotes heart disease and high blood pressure, obesity, diabetes, osteoporosis

Given all these potential threats, I see the importance of taking breaks, relaxing, praying, and reading. In the morning and evening, I take quiet time to read the Bible and ask God to guide me in my life. This relaxes me and takes away any stress that I may encounter throughout the day. God tells us not to worry or be stressed out about future events. *"Be anxious for nothing but in all prayer and supplication, let your requests be made know to God; then the peace of Christ that surpasses all understanding will guard your heart and mind."* (Philippians 4:6-7)

According to an article on *seattlepi.com*, "Stephen Covey, the best selling author of *The 7 Habits of Highly Effective People* (1989), dedicated the final segment of his book to the subject of rest and rejuvenation. In his last chapter, titled *Principles of Balanced Self-Renewal*, Covey illustrates the 'importance of regular regeneration' with the story of a man who exhausts himself trying to cut down a tree with a dull saw. 'Taking time to sharpen the saw' is what he calls the seventh habit, which 'surrounds the other habits [...] because it is the habit that makes all others possible.' Taking enough time to renew our strengths and resources is necessary to preserve and enhance the greatest asset we have, ourselves. This does not only include our physical health, but also our emotional, mental, social and spiritual well-being. Obviously, they are all intertwined and dependent on each other. Forcing ourselves to keep going when we're running on empty may be the worst thing we can do – for our work *and* ourselves.

Researchers in the relatively new field of 'psychobiology' have shown that our mind follows a certain pattern of activity and rest throughout the day. In analogy to the more familiar "circadian rhythm" (the 24 hour cycle of night and day), they call these fluctuations of the mind 'ultradian rhythms.' According to their findings: 'The mind does switch back and forth between periods of intense focusing and phases of recovery – not at the time of our choosing, but at its own volition. In other words, we are biologically programmed to take breaks and rest periods, whether we want to or not. Scientists believe that these downtimes are necessary to clean the body of metabolic waste and restore energy. Continuously and forcefully ignoring the need for rest and relaxation can lead to any number of negative consequences, such as chronic stress and many of the typical stress-related-health-effects.'"

I realize that my stress can be better controlled with the use of breaks including sleeping more. According to an article on *about.com*: "sleeping helps to reduce depression, inflammation, stress as well as improving memory and level of alertness. Lack of sleep has even been associated with obesity! Researchers have also found that people who sleep less than seven hours per night are more likely to be overweight or obese. It is thought that the lack of sleep impacts the balance of hormones in the body that affect appetite. The hormones ghrelin and leptin, important for the regulation of appetite, have been found to be disrupted by lack of sleep." Life can be stressful and busy but it is always important to get sufficient sleep. *"Life is stressful dear. That's why they say, "rest in peace."* (David Mazzucchelli, American comic book writer)

When I think about all the things I have to do prior to going to bed, I know that by getting more rest at night, I can improve my productivity and help reduce stress in my life. According to the *National Sleep Foundation*, American employees lost $18 billion in productivity during 2012 due to lack of sleep. I know that staying up until late at night to work on a project isn't healthy on a regular basis. Lack of sleep impacts my mood as well. If I get less than six hours of sleep, I feel grumpy and am less productive and efficient. As time wears on and I continue to get insufficient sleep, the problems just gets worse. In fact, a person can only live a few days on about two or three hours of sleep! Another way that sleep deficiency harms productivity is through micro sleeping. According to the *National Sleep Foundation*, roughly 37.9% of Americans fall asleep at least once during the day in a given month out of exhaustion. Micro sleeping has the potential to hurt both physically and mentally. I can impact people physically by increasing the likelihood of a car accident and mentally by downgrading the brains performance. That being said, sleep is absolutely imperative to my well-being and I make every effort to get at least 7.5 hours of sleep each night.

After a good nights sleep, I feel refreshed and any stressful events of the previous day seem like they happened a year ago. Sleep is a great stress reliever but there are others such as taking breaks and exercises. In the case of breaks, I have noticed that when I don't take breaks my mind becomes very foggy and I am unable to focus. The longer we work on a project, the greater the stress that builds up. This stress results in higher blood pressure, which increases the risk of heart attacks and strokes. Without enough breaks the stress will eventually turn into burnout and this is definitely destructive to productivity. For example, "Workplace stress costs more than $300 billion each year in health care, missed work and stress-reduction," according to an article on *proactivechange.com*. I know that if I want optimal performance from my body, I must care for it. That includes keeping stress at a minimal level as well as exercising.

I am not a fitness fanatic but I realize that if I don't exercise, I will not be as productive and will be more prone to stress. Exercising not only reduces the stress but also decreases the chances of developing unhealthy eating habits. According to an article on *livestrong.com*, these unhealthy habits include:

- Drinking to much coffee
- Eating the wrong foods
- Skipping meals
- Mindless Munching
- Forgetting Water
- Fast Food

I have personally found these things to be true especially in the case of coffee. The first thing I reach for is that tall coffee mug when I'm tired. If the first cup doesn't work, I go for a second one. In the evening I'm wired and can't go to bed thinking to myself, "No wonder!"

In order to be successful in college and to reach my future goals, I need to manage my stress but not by drinking two pots of coffee. I can manage my stress more effectively by exercising, sleeping and taking breaks. By "keeping my eye on the future," I know that taking the time to do things like exercise and sleep will be well worth the time. *"When in situations of stress we wonder if there is any more in us to give, we can be comforted to know that God, who knows our capacity perfectly, placed us here to succeed"* (Neal Maxwell, member of the Quorum of the Twelve Apostles, 1926-2004)

If I get overwhelmed and begin feeling like I will not reach my small goals and my future goals, I am reminded of Dr. Seuss – a favorite author of mine when I was young. Dr. Seuss was rejected by 27 different publishers submitting his book, *To Think I Saw It on Mulberry Street*. He didn't just give up; he kept trying and looked to other publishers and became successful. *"You will be famous as famous can be with the whole wide world watching you win on TV".* (Dr. Seuss)

Vincent Van Gogh sold only one painting during his lifetime. He may have thought he was failure but he wasn't. After his death, his paintings grew in popularity to the degree that they were selling for millions of dollars. These men didn't let those disappointments destroy them; they adapted to change. *"In times of great stress or adversity, it's always best to keep busy, to plow your anger and your energy into something positive."* (Lee Iacocca, American Businessman for Ford Motor Company)

Playing a challenging piece my piano teacher mom taught me

Chapter 24 - Do Pros Procrastinate?

A couple years ago, my parents thought it would be helpful to have a personal trainer guide me with proper weight lifting techniques and even provide additional exercises to strengthen my right arm and leg. My personal trainer, Travis, designed a difficult and personal workout routine that was to be carried out daily. At first, I was so excited about my new routine that I couldn't wait to do it every day. As the newness wore off and the difficulty increased though, I would skip days and not exercise at all. I took my eye off my future and the end goal of being strong and having symmetry in my right arm and leg. My personal trainer, Travis, pointed out that following this method, my left side would make more gains as the result of the added weight increasing my asymmetry in the process. I then proceeded to make adjustments accordingly and was able to become more symmetrical. When I thought about procrastinating, I would remind myself that my success in obtaining symmetry hinged on me remaining consistent and doing my exercises every day. *"Never put off until tomorrow what you can do the day after tomorrow."* (Mark Twain)

The concept of skipping my exercise seemed appealing at first, because I would have an extra hour in the day to do fun activities and other pressing matters. However, I came to realize the importance of making priorities and asked myself what mattered to me. Did I want to have a weaker and smaller right arm and leg or did I want to work daily at getting stronger? When I procrastinated with my exercises, I found myself getting lazy. For example, I would say to myself that I would do my exercises at nine in the morning and then wait a couple of hours and end up not doing the exercises at all. I was accomplishing nothing with my procrastination and realized the real winners work hard every day. *"You may delay, but time will not."* (Benjamin Franklin)

According to an article on *about-goal-setting.com*, there are five key negatives to procrastination:

- A feeling that a job has been left undone is bad for the morale
- Unfinished jobs leave a lot of clutter which effects our efficiency

- Putting things off means jobs accumulate and needless panic can set in
- Procrastination may be synonymous to some people with laziness and lack of interest in the job
- The job becomes more unpleasant the more you postpone it

I realized that if I developed the habit of procrastination young, I might continue the habit as an adult with disastrous consequences. For example, one time my mother, sisters and I went GameStop right about the time it was supposed to open. Since we were early, we waited. Two minutes went by then five. I stood there sweating as the sun beamed down on my brown hair watching the seconds, which seemed like minutes, go by in irritation. We ended up waiting for a half hour past opening time before the guy actually came and opened up. This wasted our day and the other customers waiting with us were annoyed and angry. Not only had they waited for the employee to open up, but now they were waiting for us as well. As soon as the untidy looking employee rang up our things, we grabbed our things and rushed out of the dimly lit store determined never to go back again. *"You cannot escape the responsibility of tomorrow by evading it today."* (Abraham Lincoln)

Though that experience was a bit disappointing and I could hear my stomach growling like a lion at the end of our wait, I learned a valuable lesson. Having a habit of procrastination might turn away my customers and, if I procrastinate at my part time job, I might create a bad reflection on my boss. My dad reminds me regularly of this verse from Matthew 5:37: *"Let your 'yes' be a 'yes' and your 'no' be a 'no'."* When I tell by boss, family member, or friend that I plan on doing a project, I need to follow through in order to build trust and I am reliable for future project. My mother also talks about this verse when she volunteers to bring a meal to a sick friend. Most often when the day comes for the meal to be delivered, there are numerous other unexpected tasks or requests and it almost seems unlikely that my mother will be able to take the meal. However, my mother says, "I said 'yes' to taking the meal and I need to let my 'yes' be a 'yes'". Amidst the busyness of that day, my mother always ends up finding the time to take the meal and has said over and over that she is the one that received the blessing from the sick friend. If I tell a friend, family member or worker, I will help, I need to let my 'yes' be a 'yes'.

In addition, procrastination may cause me to miss a deadline causing much stress in the process. During my years as a homeschooler, we had a schedule to meet with our studies. My parents allowed for a lot of freedom however, I knew if I didn't accomplish my studies, I could fall behind a grade and may not go to college. My parents wanted me to establish good study habits by having a routine and knew this would help in meeting school deadlines when I went to college.

Natascha Santos, a certified school psychologist and behavioral therapist in New York, identifies three tips can help parents promote healthy study habits with their teens as they head back to school:

"**1. Set a schedule:** Studying should be part of your student's daily routine, not something he or she tries to cram in the night before a test, Santos says. The researchers behind the report agree, advising students to parse out their study time over the course of the week, rather than letting due dates dictate their study time.

Preparing for tests ahead of time can reduce anxiety, and finishing assignments ahead of schedule can be rewarding for students, says Santos, who recommends that parents and students write due dates and major deadlines on a calendar or planner to serve as a visual reminder.

2. Eliminate distractions: Cell phones, Facebook, and TV can quickly interrupt a productive study session. Curb your temptation to tune in, text, or update their status by shutting down any unnecessary electronics during scheduled study times.

'Especially with cell phones, it's like their third eye at this point,' Santos says. 'That's such a distraction.'

Since students often need a computer to complete online assignments or type papers, Santos suggests that parents pay attention and check in with their studious teens. 'It's pretty easy to gauge if they're going onto social media sites versus typing out an essay,' she adds.

3. Break it up: Maintaining focus during a two-hour study session may be challenging, so know your teen's limits and divvy up study time accordingly, licensed psychotherapist Michelle Aycock writes in a column on the Savannah Morning Herald's website. 'Being aware of their attention span can help you structure their study time so that it will be successful,' she writes.

Parents should also set milestones for large projects or important tests such as midterms or college entrance exams, Santos, the New York-based school psychologist, notes."

"If you believe you can accomplish everything by "cramming" at the eleventh hour, by all means, don't lift a finger now. But you may think twice about beginning to build your ark once it has already started raining" (Max Brooks, author and screenwriter)

With college starting, I continue to work on maintaining small daily goals that lead up to my large goal of a doctorate in neurology. I find that these smaller goals enable me to get more done and minimize procrastination. Altogether, I believe that there are five key tips to procrastination. According to an article on *wealthforteens.com* these tips are:

"**1. Recharge Daily:** Be sure to get enough sleep and rest each day so that you have the necessary energy you need to accomplish your tasks.

2. Get a Friend Involved: It's harder to procrastinate when another person is involved. If you have a task you aren't looking forward to, invite a friend over to help you out. If you have errands to run, find a buddy who you can run errands with.

3. Reward Yourself: You're much more likely to complete that boring task if there is a dinner out or a new CD waiting for you when (and only when) the task is complete.

4. Do Things in Pieces: Procrastination often comes from feelings of overwhelm. Break tasks, even small ones, into steps so that they are manageable and provide you with a sense of direction.

5. Use Music: Turn on some fun and upbeat music and let it pump you up! 80s music and show tunes are often great pick-me-ups that will give you needed energy to tackle your tasks.

6. Prioritize: Perhaps you're procrastinating on a task because it's really not that important. Maybe you'd love to re-organize your bookshelves, but never get around to it. If it sounds like a good idea but in the end it's really not that important to you, don't let it hang over your head.

7. Get in Touch with the End Result: Before you begin a task or project that has high procrastination potential; get in touch with the outcome. When the task is finished, what will that mean to you? What will be better in life as a result?"

I had to learn the hard way, that procrastination is never helpful in the long run. With my exercises, I ended up not making as much progress as I might have if I would of avoided procrastination. I was sad that my arm wasn't catching up with my left one as quickly but it was my fault and I could blame no one else. That being said, I believe that whatever end goal I have can be better achieved without procrastination *"My advice is to never do tomorrow what you can do today. Procrastination is the thief of time."* (Charles Dickens)

Thanking God for a strong mind and body.

Chapter 25 - Leaving Life with a Legacy

When I make decisions and face challenges, I think about what others think and what legacy I will leave behind when I die. I frequently ask myself: " What do I want to be remembered for and what impression do I want to leave with the people I know?" My goal is to live a life worth living and though I am young and death seems distant or almost non-existent, it exists and I should entertain the thought that I won't be here forever.

My Uncle George Huffaker, for whom I am named, recently passed away. He lived a quiet, one would think non-influential, life. Uncle George, a farmer in the mountains of Kentucky, lived in a 1800 square foot house with no air conditioner. His simple life consisted of caring for a brother, farming and attending the local Baptist Church. His life was far simpler than the life of someone always in the headlines like Donald Trump. However, when I closely examined my Uncle George's life, I was surprised and shocked. Uncle George's history was very different from what I had initially imagined. In fact, my uncle had similar goals to mine. He wanted to be a doctor. He studied and worked hard, then finally went off to college, where he even met Billy Graham. Just as my uncle settled into college life, he received a disturbing message. His dad had passed away and his mother was sick. Uncle George made a life changing decision directed by God. He left medical school to care for his mother and the farm. Uncle George spent the rest of his life watching over his mother, until she died, and a sick brother. He also used his intelligence to continue farming, growing the family business by buying acres and acres of land. Uncle George then set up oil drills and began another business that prospered the family. After his death, many members of the community told us stories of Uncle George's generosity and assistance he gave others so they too would be successful. My Uncle George left a Christian legacy that touched so many.

I hope my life will touch others when I am young and old as well. I always need to be ready for our ultimate home in heaven. When I was in grade school, I told my parents "We live in a garage". My mom looked at me with shocked eyes, "George, we live in a lovely, large home." I looked at my mom and said, "Mom, this is a garage. Heaven is our real home." My mom smiled and said, "George, you are so wise." *"You must be ready, for the Son of Man is coming at an hour you do not expect."* (Matthew 24:44)

An article on *lifeteen.com* inspired me to live my life as a legacy for others: "Everyone knows fun people who know how to have a great time on Earth. Some of those people live as if Earth is the last stop. It's vital to Christian living to be joyful here on Earth, but to remember also that this is a journey, and Heaven is the destination. When you pass away, people will be inspired by the joy and hope you had. They'll be moved by the way you chose eternal sanctification over immediate satisfaction. They'll be challenged by the way you loved them, because you saw that Heaven was their destination too, and you wanted to help them get there. They will think about you, and end up thinking about Jesus.

They'll reflect on the ways they saw Christ in you. Even further, they'll reflect on the ways you saw Christ in them. They'll remember the way you treated them with respect and dignity. They'll remember the way you smiled at them and brightened their day. Those moments when you had every reason to frown but chose joy anyway will inspire them to be joyful.

Let your actions reflect honesty, faith, and virtue. Use words that build up the Kingdom. Conduct yourself with prudence and patience. Live in the hope and the promises of Jesus Christ. When you are long gone, the hope and promises of Jesus will remain. Become a saint. When people think of you, they will praise God. That's the best kind of legacy you can leave."

As a teenager, I usually do not dwell on death since it seems I will live forever. At the age of 16, it seems like I won't be 80 for centuries to come. It's hard to imagine that I may be a short, white haired, frail looking man in the not so distant future. The thought of this, however, makes me appreciate life more and pursue a better relationship with God. My grandmother, who will turn 90, lived with us for a few months. She talked about her teenage years as if they were yesterday. My grandmother's face is still beautiful but with wrinkles. She reflected regularly on what it was like to live with 11 siblings. Her parents, farmers in Kentucky, encouraged the girls and boys to go to college. My grandmother earned her college tuition by teaching a semester in a small country school in the mountains. She rode her horse up to the school and prepared the wood stove so the students would stay warm. My grandmother reminisced about how well behaved the students and how beautiful the mountain trees and flowers were during her years as a schoolteacher.

My grandmother would also say to me, "Heaven is going to be amazing, filled with all sorts of people. Think of the people throughout the generations," she said often. My grandmother is not afraid to die and looks forward to seeing Jesus. Death isn't something I should be afraid of if I have led a meaningful life. In fact, it is something to look forward to if I believe in the Lord. *"The fear of death follows from the fear of life. A man who lives fully is prepared to die at any time."* (Mark Twain)

After I die, heaven awaits and it will be much more splendid than anything that the world has to offer. However, I want to depart knowing that I have enriched the lives of others. The memories that I create are the most important aspect of the legacy I leave behind. *"The life of the dead is placed in the memory of the living."* (Cicero) Life is not about amassing wealth or being famous because, in the end, these things will be meaningless. Nobody will remember that I had a sports car or large home nor will they care. The possessions I leave behind will not pass the test of time. *"No matter how many toys we amass we leave them behind when we die, just as we leave a broken environment, an economy that only benefits the richest, and a legacy of empowering greed over goodness. It is now time to commit to following a new path."* (John Perkins, author)

I want my life to enrich the lives of other people and encourage them in their spiritual walk. It is my duty to shine the love of Christ in the world. By applying the Bible's principals in my life, I can become successful both spiritually and physically as well as enriching the lives of others with the truth of the Bible. *"Our days are numbered. One of the primary goals in our lives should be to prepare for our last day. The legacy we leave is not just in our possessions, but in the quality of our lives. What preparations should we be making now? The greatest waste in all of our earth, which cannot be recycled or reclaimed, is our waste of the time that God has given us each day."* (Billy Graham)

My life's mission is to bring joy, inspiration, and even healing into the lives of others with a career in medicine. One day, I will have the pleasure of seeing the golden gates of Heaven open up and view the lush landscape and buildings that sparkle like diamonds. I look forward to always seeing the sun shining in the sky, beaming its rays on the warm soil and will be thrilled to get started living life in paradise. When I am finished on this earth, I desire to hear God say, *"Well done, good and faithful servant."* (Matthew 25:23)

My family is my greatest support team!

Chapter 26 - Reflection on The Projection of The Long Term

As I look back on the challenges I have gone through such as a weak and small right leg and arm, a tightened fist, trouble learning and talking, I know with the invisible hand of the Lord guiding me, I can conquer anything. *"I can do all things through Christ who strengthens me."* (Philippians 4:13)

I cannot, however, become complacent and think that I have arrived physically, spiritually, and mentally with education to the finish line. I have to continue to push myself to grow in all areas of my life. After reaching my initial goals, I continue by making more goals guided by God. I have reached the goal of getting into college, having a 4.0 GPA, and achieving an ACT score that provides me with free college. I continue to work on the next goal of graduating with a 4.0 and then push on toward a masters and doctorate specializing in neurology. It will be hard. I will want to give up, but through prayer, encouragement from friends and family and hard work, I can reach these goals. *"Get going. Move forward. Aim High. Plan a takeoff. Don't just sit on the runway and hope someone will come along and push the airplane. It simply won't happen. Change your attitude and gain some altitude. Believe me, you'll love it up here."* (Donald Trump)

My hope for this book is to encourage other teens that are facing physical challenges and even learning challenges. As mentioned in previous chapters, I had trouble learning in a traditional classroom. It was humiliating not knowing a certain topic when everyone got it down cold. The state of my education got slightly better when I started homeschooling but I still spent years struggling to read an hour a day by myself and getting stuck on every other page of my schoolwork. I was finally able to develop a love for learning and increased my academic performance thanks to my parents encouragement and praying to God for His guidance. I needed it too becomes there were times when the next grade seemed as far away as it does graduating from college in a four year olds mind.

Physically, I felt like the odd teen out with my arm and leg on the right side much smaller than the opposite for a very long time. I still have that symmetry issue and work to improve my physical appearance. I sometimes get depressed about my challenges wondering why God created me this way. However, I always cheer up when I realize that God has big plans for me even with my challenges. I can achieve whatever I want with Gods help and a good work ethic. I realize that my challenges will only be a disability if I let them. *"With God, all things are possible."* (Matthew 19:26)

I welcome all emails to george.alan.day@gmail.com and would gladly help guide you in your challenges by sharing wisdom that helped me overcome Cerebral Palsy. I look forward to encouraging teens and even parents of children with special needs. In my life, I see how everything happens for a reason, and I know my challenges as a child and teen occurred to show the greatness of God. By combining God's grace with the discipline of hard work, great goals that others thought impossible will be achieved. *"With man this is impossible, but with God all things are possible."* (Matthew 19:26)

My friend and sister, Emily and me.

Bibliography

"About the Purpose Driven Life"/ nod/ purposedriven/
http://purposedriven.com/books/pdbooks/#purpose

Adolescent and School Health/ Childhood Obesity Facts"/ n.d./ CDC</
http://www.cdc.gov/healthyyouth/obesity/facts.htm

"Agenda: Grinding America Down"/movieguide.org/
http://www.movieguide.org/reviews/movie/agenda-grinding-america
down.html

"Aggression"/18Apr2006/
http://www.mtv.com/news/articles/1528932/study-rap-lovers-more-
prone-frug-se.jhtml

"Alcohol Under-Age Drinking"/\pvamu.edu/
http://www.pvamu.edu/pages/2315.asp

Andrade Elizabeth/ 27Nov2012/ "the value of chores"/ Gametown
Avenue Parents/
http://gametownavenueparents.com/2012/11/the-value-of-chores/

Amerman Don/8Jan2012/"Does Going To Sleep Earlier Makes You
Feel Better"/Livestrong/
http://www.livestrong.com/article/552907-does-going-to-sleep-earlier-
make-you-feel-better

"Athens"/2012/ http://en.wikipedia.org/wiki/Athens/

Baach Eryln/n.d./ "The Causes of Poverty in Mexico/ eslbee.com"/
http://www.eslbee.com/causes_of_poverty_in_mexico.htm

Barbour Scott/n.d./ "The Effects of Alcohol on a Teen's Body"/
ehow.com/
http://www.ehow.com/info_8111664_effects-alcohol-teens-body.html

Bono Edward de/ n.d./ "Power of Perception"/de Bono Consulting/
http://www.debonoconsulting.com/power-of-perception.asp

"Burton Jonathan/14May2007/"What teens need to know about money"/MarketWatch/ http://articles.marketwatch.com/2007-05-14/finances/3078111_credit-cars-budget-wall-mon

"Cannabinoids"/n.d./Washington.edu/ http://adai.washington.edu/marijuana/facts/cannabiniods.htm

Castillo Michelle/ 3Jul2012/ "One in four teens admits to sexting, study finds"/CBS New/ http://www.cbsnews.com/8301-504763_162_57465730-10391704/one-in-four-teens-admit-to-s

Casteele John/ n.d. /"What Ballet Does for Football"/Demand Media/ azcentral.com/ http://healthyliving.azcentral.com/ballet-football-1747.html

Cavalli Ernest/ 27Dec2007/ "Doctor Claims Gaming Causes Brain Damage"/Wired/ http://www.wired.com/gamelife/2207/12/doctor-claims-g/

Amanda/ 15March2011 /"For Teens, Acne Impacts Self Esteem"/ http://www.myhealthnewsdaily.com/1054-severe-acne-impacts-self-Chan-esteem.html

Chan Amanda /n.d./ "Pet Health Benefits: Study Shows Dogs and Cats May Make Kids"/Huffpost Healthy Living/ http://www.huffingtonpost.com/2012/07/09/health-benefits-pets-respiratory-infection-healthier-

Clark Valerie/n.d./"The bad Effects of Rap Music on Teenagers"/eHow/ http://www.ehow.com/facts_4914950_bad-effects-rap-music-teenagers.html

"College Student Employment"/n.d./The Condition of Education/ http://nces.ed.gov/programs/coe/indicator_csw.asp

Cornett Matthew/ n.d./ "Cultivate a Grateful Attitude in Your Teens"/TheParentLink/
http//www.wingsoffaith.com/userFiles/1466/1108_-_jsm.pdf

Curtis Browning [director] "Agenda" [Motion picture]
AgendaDocumentary.com

Chemistry/ Brad R. Batdorf/BJU press/ 2009

"Cyber Bullying Statistics"/n.d./ Bullying Statistics/
http://www.bullyingstatistics.org/content/cyber-bulling-statistics.html

Daily Media Use Among Children And Teens Up Dramatically From Five Years Ago/ 20January2010/Kaiser Family Foundation/
http://www.kff.org/entmedia012010nr.cfm

Davis Jeanie/n.d./ "5 Ways Pets Can Improve Your Health"
http://www.webmd.com/hypertension-high-blood-pressure/features/health-benefits-of-pets

Davis Warren/n.d./ "Five things everybody needs to know about materialism"/ Generally Thinking/
http://generallythinking.com/five-thingd-everybody-needs-to-know-about-materialism-2/

Dizon Kristin/30Jan2004 / "World's fittest man says if he could get in shape, so can you"/Seattlepi.com/
http://www.seattlepi.com/lifestyle/health/article/World-s-fittest-man-says-if-he-could-ge

Donald Trump/Forbes /Sep2012/
http://www.forbes.com /profile/Donald-trump/

"Dr. Dobson's Principals od Discipline"/n.d./Dr. James Dobson's familytalk/
http://drjamesdobson.org/Solid-Answers/Answers?a=elabe8e73-170c-45e3-8d73-76557db38d085

Dr. Pepper Nutritional Information/n.d./ LiveStrong.com/

http://www.livestrong.com/thedailyplate/nutrition-calories/food/dr.pepper/

"Drug Abuse"/15Jan2013/The New York Times/
http://health.nytimes.com/health/guides/specialtopic/drug-abuse/overview.html

"DrugFacts: Marijuana"/Dec2012/drugabuse.gov/
http://www.drugabuse.gov/publications/drugfacts/marijuans

Dube Ryan/ 29Oct2008 "History of U.S. Presidential Hobbies"/Articlesbase/
http://www.articlebase.com/history-of-us-presidential hobbies- 620721

Ebersole John/8Aug2012/ "Why a College Degree"/Forbs/
http://www.forbs.com/sites/johnebersole/2012/08/why-a-college-degree/

"11 Shocking Facts About Teens and Drug Use"/n.d./
Dosomething.com/
http://www.dosomething.org/actnow/tipsandtools/11-shocking-facts-about-teens-and-drug-use

"Eliminate Curse Words From Your Vocabulary"/n.d./Wired to Grow/
http://wiredtogrow.com/eliminate-curse/

Estrella Espie/ n.d./ "Benefits of Music Education"/About.com/
http://musiced.about.com/od/beginnersguide/a/pinst.htm

Erickson Rose/n.d./"How Nutrition Effects The Brain of Adolescents"/
Livestrong/
http://www.livestrong.com<article/364298-how-nutrition-affects-the-brain-of-adolescents/

Facts and Statistics/n.d./ "MBNBD Make A Sound For A Voice Unheard"/
http://www.makebeatsnotbeatdowns.org/facts_new.html

"Facts on American Teens' Sex and Reproductive Health"/n.d./ Guttmatcher Institutehttp://www.guttmacher.org/pubs/FB-ATSRH.html

"Fast Food Nutrition: Junk Foods Effect on Your Body"/n.d./Fitday/ http://www.fitday.com/fitness-articles/nutrition/healthy-eating/fast-food-nutrition-junk-foods-eff

"Fitness Basics: Swimming is for Everyone"/n.d./ Samatoro Barbara Russi/
WebMD
http://www.webmd.com/fitness-exercise/guide/fitness-basics-swimming-is-for-everyone

5 Effective Work Habits For Fresh Graduates"/n.d./Career-Success-For-
Newbies/
http://www.career-success-for-newbies.com/effective-work-habits.html

"5 Keys to Financial Success"/1Sep2010/Rodgers & Associates/ http://rodgers-associates.com/5-keys-to-financial-success/

Gannett Washington Bureau/n.d./ "On Social Security"/ USA Today/ http://usatoday30.usatoday.com/news/political issues/socialsecurity

"Grateful Teens May Have Less Risk for Depression"/ 5Aug2012/University of Utah Health Care/ http://healthcare.utah.edu/healthlibrary/related/doc.php?type=6&id=662 90

"Gratitude Healthy:10 Reasons Why Being Thankful is Good For You"/22Nov2012/ HuffPost Healthy Living/ http://www.huffingtonpost.com/2012/11/22/gratitude-healthy-benefits_n_2147182.html - slide=1770

Gaylord Chris/16Sep2008/"By the numbers: teens and video games"/TheChristianScience Monitor/ http://www.csmonitor.com/Innov

Gilani Nadia/17Oc2011/"Bad language in video games and on TV linked to aggression in teenagers"/
http://ww.dailymail.co.uk/newss/article-250159/Bad-language-video-games-TV-linked-aggresion

Gikerson Luke/n.d./ "Teens and Porn:10 Stats You Need to Know"/Breaking Free Blog/
http://www.covenanteyes.com/2010/08/19/teens-and-porn-10-stats-your-need-to-know/

Glang Vivian/12June2012/ "11 Homeless People Who Became Rich and Famous"/ Business Insider/
http://www.businessinsider.com/formerly-homless-people-who-became-famous-2012-67op

Gordon Merry/n.d./ "From Cursive to Cursor: The Death of Handwriting"education.com/
http://www.education.comemagazine/article/cursive-cursor-death-handwriting/

Groenewald Andrea/n.d/ "Learn to See Yourself as God Sees You"/Powertochange/
http://powertochange.com/experience/life/holiness/

Gustafson Timi/27March2010/ "The Importance of Taking Breaks"/ /seattlepi
http://blog.seattlepi.com/timigustafsonrd/2010/03/27/the-importance-of-taking-breaks/

Gustafson Rod/15Oc2007/"What Parents Need to Know About TV's In Children's Bedrooms"/parentstv.org/
http://parentstv.org/PTC/publications/rgcolumns/2007/1015.asp

Harris Anna/9Aug2012/"Keeping the faith on campus"/World on campus/
http://www.worldoncampus.com/2012/08/keeping_faith_on_campus

Harmon Emily/11Oc2007/"Improve Your Christian Life by Finding an Accountability Partner/Yahoo/

http://voices.yahoo.com/improve-christian-life-finding-accountability-586402

"Health Benefits of Exercise"/ 2010/ Nutristrategy/
http://www.nutristrategy.com/health.htm

"Healthier"/7Sep2012/huffingtonpost.com/
http://www.huffingtonpost.com/2012/07/09/health-benefits-respiratory-infection-healthier-

Herr Norman/ n.d./ "Television Statistic"/ The Sourcebook For Teaching Science/
http://www.csun.edu/science/health/docs/tv&health.html

Hollister Danielle/n.d./ "Top 25 Leadership Quotations"
http://ezinearticles.com/? Top-25-Leadership-Quotations&id=4849

Houghton Kristen/n.d./ "Dreams Have No Age Limit: Famous People Who Started Late"/Huffpost Healthy Living/ 4June2010
http://www.huffingtonpost.com/kristen-houghton/dreams-have-no-age-
- limit_b_525358

"How Music Affects Us and Promotes Health"/ n.d./ eMedExpert
http://www.emedexpert.com/tips/music.shtml

"How Teens Can Become Millionaires"/
12March2010/daveramsey.com/
http:///www.daveramsey.com/article/how-teens-can-become-
millionaires/lifeandmoney_kidsandmo

Javitch David/ 9Dec2009 /"10 Characteristics of Superior Leaders"
http://www.entrepeneur.com/article/204248

John Briggs/ "Financial Statistics of College Grads vs. Non-
Grads"/eHow/
http://www.ehow.com/about_6128503_financial-college-grads-vs-non-grad-vs-non-grads.html

"Joni Eareckson Tada"/ 2Jan2013 /Wikipedia.org/2Jan2013/

http://www.wikipedia.org/w/index.php?title=Joni_Eareckson_Tada&action=history

"Josiah"/6June2012/ Wikipedia /http://en.wikipedia.org/wiki/Josiah

Jurado Anthony/ 7Feb2010/ "7 Insane Ways Music Affects The Body"(According to Science)/Cracked.com/
http://www.cracked.com/article_18405_7-insane-ways-music-affects-body-according-to-science.h

Kolle Amber/n.d./ "Rap Music and the Teenage World"/
http://www.wright.edu/cola/Dept/eng/blakelock/rockweb2/rockpgs/R99/rapeffects2.htm

Latumahina Donald/ n.d./"Time Quotes: 66 Best Time Management Quotes"/ life optimizer/
http://www.lifeoptimizer.org/2007/03/08/66-best-quotes-on-time-management

Lawson Jake/ 11Aug2011/ "People-Pleasing-Personality"/Livestrong/
http://www.livestrong.com/article/14669-people-pleasing-personality/

"List of countries by vehicle per capita"/18Dec2012Wikipedia/18Dec2012/
http://en.wikipedia.org/wiki/List_of_countries_by_vehicle_per_capita

"Low Self-Esteem"/n.d./UTSC/
http://www.utsc.utoronto.ca/~wellness/counclling_lse.html

Lynn Diana/12May2011/"Healthy/Food Statistics"/
http://www.livestrong.com/article/439572-healthy-food-statistics/

Marks Diana/ 15Jan2011/"Dairy & Sinus Infections"/Livestrong/
http://www.livestrong.com/article/357278-dairy-sinus-infections/

Marks Linda/ 2006/ "The Health Impact of Love and Fear"/Heart Power/
http://www.healingpower.com/love-fear.html

Maganiellio Jim/ 4June2010 / "Health and Well-Being; Bottling up emotions carries health risks"/
http://www.neburyportnews.com/lifestyle/x1996913112/Health-and-Well-Being-Bottling-up-em

Markham Dr. Laura/ n.d./ "Structure: Why Kids Need Routines/
http://www.ahaparenting.com/parenting-tools/family-life/structure-routines

"Materialistic beliefs causing kids depression"/n.d./Mail Online/
http://www.dailymail.com.uk/health/article-172017/Materialist-beliefs-causing-kids-depression.htm

Maxwell Dr. John/ 9April2009/ "The Best Leaders Are Listeners"/Grace/
http://graceattitude.wordpress.com/2009/04/09/the-best-leaders-are-listeners/

Miller Victoria / 14Nov2009 /"Celebrities Who Have Used Positive Affirmations to Get Rich"/ Yahoo/
http://voices.yahoo.com/celebrities-used-positive-affirmations-to-4866086.html?cat=3

Mintle Dr. Linda/25March2010/"Family"/CBN/
http://blogs.cbn.com/familymatters/archive/2010/03/25/men-who-do-housework-have-happier-

Pandy Karen / 27Sep2011/ "Thomas Edison's Inventions"/ Buzzle/
http://www.buzzle.com/articles/thomas-edison-inventions.html

Parker-Pope Tara/4March2008 "One Eyed Invader in the Bedroom"/nytimes.com/
/http://www.nytimes.com/2008/03/04/health/04well.html

Paul Mark/ 9Nov2012/"Lindsay Lohan Banned from Hotel: Other stars Who've been Banned"/Yahoo/
http://omg.yahpp.com/news/lindsey-lohan-banned-hotel-other-stars-whove-banned-210000445.htlm

"PeerPressure"/n.d. humanillnesses.com/
http://www.humanillnesses.com/Behavioral-Health-Ob-Sea/Peer-Pressure.html#b

"Peer Pressure, Cliques, and Gangs"/ n.d./ sites.google.com/
http://sites.google.com/site/peerpressureclicksgangs/peerpressure-definition

Philips Katharine/ 23Feb2006 "Clinical features of body dysmorphic disorder in adolescents and adults"/
http://www.ncbi.nlm.nih.gov/pmc/articles/PMCI1592052

"Physical Activity Facts"/n.d./ CDC Facts"/CDC/
http://www.cdc.gov/healthyouth/physicalactivity/facts.htm

Pierrre Colleen/ n.d./"Diet is Key"/ Parents/
http://www.parents.com/toddlers-preschooolers/health/asthma/ anti-aging-diet

Pike R./ n.d./ "side effects for users of porn"/ Fight Pornography/
Addiction/6July2009 http://abattleplan.com/2009/07/side-effects-users-porn/

"Power of Visualization-The Secrets to Jimmy Carrey,Michael Jordan and Tiger Wood's Success"/ n.d./ silvalifesystem.com/
http://www.Silvalifesystem.com/articles/visualization-techniques/power-of-visualization/

"Practical Life Skills"/27March2011/aaimsschool.com/
http://http://www.aaimsschool.com/practical-life-skills-at-aaims/

"Procrastination-Five Negative Results"/n.d./about-goal- setting.com/
http://www.about-goal-setting.com/time-management-guide/16-procrastination.html

Quaglia Dom/28Nov2012/ "Live For Heaven"/lifeteeen/
http://lifeteen.com/live-for-heaven-legacy/

"Report: Was Demi Moore Smoking K2 Spice?"/ 30Jan2012/ extratv.com/
http://www.extratv.com/2012/01/30/report-was-demi-moore-smoking-k2- spice/

"Riches To Rags: 10 Celebrities Who Went Broke"/ 23March2012 Cosmoloan/
http://www.cosmoloan.com/loans/from-riches-to-rags-10-celebrities-who-went-broke.html

Sasson Remez/"The Benefits of Peace of Mind and Tranquility"/ successconcious.com/
http://www.successconcious.com/peace_benefits.htm

Schumacher Robin/ "What is Moral Relativism?"/ carm.org/
http://carm.org/moral-relativism

Scott Elizabeth/ 29April2012/ "Stress and Nutrition: The Link Between Stress and Nutrition Deficencies"/About.com/
http://stress.about.com/od/dietsandsupplements/a/stressnutrition.htm

Sefcik Lisa/ 5Dec2011/"Warning! Teen Dating Hurts"/EssayForum/
http://www.easyforum.com/writing-feedback-3/group-essay-warning-teen-dating-hurts-34176/

Shute Nancy/ 5Feb2008/"Drugs and Alcohol and Your Kids Music"/ HealthUSnews/
http://www.healthy.usnews.com/health-news/blogs/onparenting/2008/02/05/ drugs-and-alcohol-and-y

Shea Sydney/15Nov2011/ "Textually active: Sexting and depression among teens are linked, study says"/The Daily Free Press/
http://dailyfreepress.com/2011/11/15/textually-active-sexting-and-depression-among-teens-are

"Student Credit & Debit Statatistics"/n.d./Credit.com/
http://www.credit.com/press/statistics/students-credit-and-debt-statistics.html

Sifferlin Alexandra/n.d./"Too much TV linked with weaker kids"/CNN health/
http://www.cnn.com/2012/07/16/health/tv-overuse-weaker-kids/index.html

"6 Downsides of Perfection"/n.d./Personal Excellence/
http://personalexcellence.co/blog/6-downsides-of-perfectionism/

"Sleeping Disorder Statistics"/ 2July2012/Statistic Brain/
http://www.statisticbrain.com/sleeping-disorder-statistics

Societal Attitudes toward Options for Troubled Teen"/n.d./Teen Suicide Statistics/
http://www.teendepression.org/related/teen-suicide-statistics/

Smith Melinda/n.d./ "Stress Symptoms, Signs and Causes"/helpguide.org/
http://www.helpguide.org/mental/stress_signs.htm

Smith Timothy/ 25April2003/ "The Seven Cries of Today's Teens"/
http://www.crosswalk.com/family/parenting/teens/the-seven-cries-of-cries-of-todays-teens-1197166.htm

Snelling Andrew/ 7Dec2007/"High and Dry Sea Creatures"/Answers/
http://www.answerssingesis.org/articles/am/v3/n1/high-dry-sea-creatures

Spivack Jill/ 27Oc2009/"Save Your Marriage-Get Your Children to Sleep"/
www.momlogic.com
http://www.momlogic.com/2009/save_your_marriage_get_your_child_to_sleep.php

"Stability, Not Marriage, Key to Kids' Happiness"/ n.d./ Marks Psychiatry/
file://localhost/http/:marksphysicatry.com:stability-not-marriage-key-to-kids-happiness

"Statistics"/n.d./English.Is.Enough/
http://www.enough.org/inside.php?tag=statistics

"Statistics on Alcohol and Driving"/ n.d. /AnapolSwartz Attorneys At Law/
http://www.analpolschwartz.com/practices/liquor-liability/statistics.asp

Statistics On Teens/ SoundVision/
SoundVision.com/http://www.soundvision.com/info/teens/stat.asp

STD Statistics and Information about STD testing/n.d./ SafeLab Centre/
http://www.safelabcentre.com/std-statistics.html

Sticbich Mark/8May2008/ "Top 10 Health Benefits of a Good Nights Sleep"/About.com/
/http://longevity.about.com/od/lifelongenergy/tp/healthy_sleep.htm

Tanglao Leezel/ 23Aug2010/"Back to School: Healthy Sleep Habits"/
abcnews.com/
http://abcnews.go.com/GMA/healthy-sleep-habits-kids-back-school/story?id=11458225

"Teenage brothers charged with killing NJ girl 12"/ 9Nov2012/Yahoo 2012/
http://news.yahoo.com/teenage-brothers-charged-killing-nj-girl-12-2205003810

"Teens' Alcohol Problems"/n.d./ alcoholcostcalculator.com/
http://www.alcoholcostcalculator.org/kids/teens/print-teens.php

"Teen Driving Statstics"/ n.d./ rmelia/
http://www.rmila.org/auto/teens/Teen_Driving_Statistics.asp

"Teen Peer Pressure: Statistics and Facts"/n.d./ Teen Peer Pressure/Family First Aid http:www.familyfirstaid.org/peer-pressure.html

"Teen Statistics"/ n.d. /canyoure18.com http://www.canyour18.com/23

"Teen Smoking Statistics"/n.d./ TeenHelp.com/
http://www.teenhelp.com/teenhealth/teen-smoking-statistics.html

"The Benefits of Time Management: What Are They?"/n.d./ Discover Time Management/
  http://www.discover-time-management.com/benefits-of-time-management.html

"The Candy Meth Myth Kids and Candy Drugs"/ 4Aug2010/ Candy Professor/
http://candyprofessor.com/2010/08/04/senate-protects-american-children-from-candy-c

"The Danger of Muscle Imbalances and the Importance of Symmetry"/
n.d./ Marks Daily Apple/
http://www.marksdailyapple.com/muscle-imbalances/#axzzz2FaffxMqy

"The Truth About Teens and Credit Cards"/3Aug2009/daveramsey.com/
http://daveramsey.com/article/the-truth-about-teens-and-credit-cards/

"The Value of Mentoring"/ n.d./ mentor/
http://www.mentoring.org/about_mentor/value_of_mentoring

"37 Percent of Employers Use Facebook To Ore-Screen Applications, New Study Says"/20April2012/
http://www.huffingtonpost.com/2012/04/20/employers-use-facebook-to-pre-screen-application_n

"Tobacco, Smoking and Nicotine Addiction Statistics and facts"/n.d./ MyAddiction.com/
http://www.myaddiction.com/education/articles/tobacco_statistics.html

"Top paying jobs" Yahoo 2012/
http://finance.yahoo.com/news/top-paying-jobs.html

"Too Much Texting?"/ 27May2009 The New York Times Assesses the impact of text messaging on health"/ Mlive

http://blog.mlive.com/>right_fit/2009/05/too_much_texting_the_new_y
ork.html

Voge Wilf/ Dec2007 "Management by Fear: Does it Really
Work?"/executivebrief.com/
http://www.executivebrief.com/article/management-by-fear-does-it-
really-work/

Vivo Megan/ n.d./"girls learn differently"/publicaffairs.ubc.ca/
http://www.publicaffairs.unc.ca/2010/03/04/perfectionism-and-youth-
suicide/

"Warning: Real Estate Investors Don't make These 7 Deadly Mistakes
That Made Donald Trump Bankrupt"/n.d./Secret2Money.com/
Secrets2Money.com/http://www.secrets2money.com/Warning-Real-
Estate-Investors-Dont-Make-These-7-deadly

William Chen/14Aug2010/ "Ten Easy Ways to Overcome
Procrastination"/ WealthForTeens/
http://www.wealthforteens.com/teen-personal-growth/10-easy-ways-
to-overcome-procrastination/

Weissmann Jordan /22Jun2012/ "How Many Students Can Actually
Work Their Way Through School"/The Atlantic/
http://www.theatlantic.com/business/archieve/2012/06/how-many-
students-can-actually

"What challenges did Mother Teresa face?"/n.d./Wiki answers/
http://wikianswers.com/Q/What_challenges_did_Mother_Teresa_face

"What is Kinesiology Used For?"/KinesiologyConnection/
http://www.kinesiology.com.au/what-is-kinesiology-used-for

"Who and Save the Children"/ 30August2011/Newborn death decreases
but account for higher share of global child deaths''/ World Health
Organization/
http://www.who.int/medicacentre/news/release/2011/newborn_deaths_
20110830/en/inde

"Why 3% of Harvard MBAs Make Ten Times as Much as the Other 97% Combined"/ Personal Development Training with SidSavara/ http://sidsavara.com/personal-productivity/why-3-of-harvard-mbas-ten-times-as-much-as

William Beach/8Feb2012/"The 2012 Index of Dependence on Government/ The Heritage Foundation"/ http://www.heritage.org/research/reports/2012/02/2012-index-of-dependence-on-government

Zorn Eric/ 3Jun2012/ "Zimmerman back behind bars for lying about money" Chicago Tribune/ http://blogs.chicagotribune.com/news_columnists_ezorn/2012/06/zimmerman-back-beh

19342497R00099

Made in the USA
Charleston, SC
18 May 2013